Praise for *The Resi*

T0282248

"Brian Molitor has done it again! *The Resilient Lea*
book that delves into the qualities that define true leadership."
—**Brian Pruitt**, Founder, The Power of Dad

"Brian uses personal experiences and draws from several other leaders to bring concrete lessons on facing storms with resiliency to stay the course and reach your goals."
—**Barry Robinson**, Vice President of Business Development, UTIL Auditors

"*The Resilient Leader* is a relevant and practical guide for leaders in any industry. Whether in healthcare, finance, church or even your own household, Brian Molitor presents an easy-to-review guide to support leaders."
—**Stephen Idzior**, Practice Manager, MYMichigan Health

"If you are currently in a leadership position or aspire to be, I highly recommend this book. It is filled with stories of experienced leaders grounded in balanced perspectives on the values of life and faith."
—**George Aultman**, Vice President of Strategic Development, Vantage Plastics

"*The Resilient Leader* provides a wealth of wisdom from diverse leaders who share their journeys, triumphs, and setbacks. Brian Molitor's ability to capture these narratives with authenticity and depth makes this book a compelling read."
—**Jim O'Brien**, Vice President, Michigan Brand

"This book is not just a guide—it is a source of comfort and motivation for anyone navigating the complexities of leadership."
—**Lisa Killey**, Assistant Dean of Student and Faculty Affairs,
Central Michigan University

"*The Resilient Leader* is a must-read for those in any type of leadership role! Brian has done an outstanding job encapsulating the key principles and qualities all leaders need to survive and overcome storms."
—**Karla Mathis**, President, National House of Hope

"I believe *The Resilient Leader* is a great primer for budding leaders. This is the type of sage wisdom and how-to advice for leadership that I have grown to expect from Brian Molitor."
—**D. Ernest Bedford**, CW02, United States Marine Corp [Retired]

"*The Resilient Leader* is a great reminder about what's important in life. It was inspiring and a great read!"

—**Jerry Stewart**, President, Balanced Biological Solutions

"*The Resilient Leader* provides clarity on how we can enjoy today and stay strong for the journey that lies before us."

—**Kathy Allbee**, Founder, Released to Reign Ministry

"Brian has done it again, providing a road map for improving your personal health and your organizational health. A great read!"

—**Ed Bruff**, CEO, Covenant HealthCare [Retired]

"Brian Molitor has written a comprehensive, strategic plan for victory in both a leader's professional as well as personal life. By applying the wisdom of this book, readers will acquire the skill and the resilience to "bounce back" from life's many hits…like a new tennis ball!"

—**John "Barney" Barnes**, CDR U.S. Navy [Retired] & Former Chief of Staff, Dorchester County Sheriff's Office

"Concise and intensely practical with many real life examples, *The Resilient Leader* meets leaders right at their point of need."

—**Jim Cross**, Dow Corning, Inc. [Retired]

"*The Resilient Leader* continues Brian's legacy of wisdom and the practical application of complex concepts. A must-read to help one live their fullest life and develop their innate leadership potential."

—**Kevin Birchmeier**, COO, Covenant HealthCare

"The stories within these pages will serve as encouragement to anyone who has faced the challenges of leading with integrity and resilience."

—**Rhonda Sciortino**, Founder, Successful Survivors Foundation

"What a timely book as we see leaders stepping down from exhaustion or moral failure. I recommend this book to every leader who has ever considered 'quitting.'"

—**Ronald Ives, Senior Pastor**, The Potter's House Family Worship Center & co-founder, The Potter's House Global Network

"Crucial connections and relationships were of pivotal importance in my leadership experiences and the lessons in this book underscore keys to resilience for leaders and staff alike. Well done!"

—**Carol M. Stoll**, RN, Director, St. Luke's Hospital

THE RESILIENT LEADER

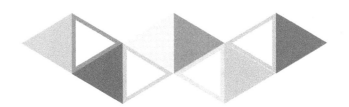

Lessons in Navigating through
Crisis and Opportunity

BRIAN D. MOLITOR

Hatherleigh Press is committed to preserving
and protecting the natural resources of the earth.
Environmentally responsible and sustainable practices are
embraced within the company's mission statement.

Visit us at www.hatherleighpress.com.

THE RESILIENT LEADER

Library of Congress Cataloging-in-Publication
Data is available upon request.

ISBN: 978-1-961293-12-0

Printed in the United States

10 9 8 7 6 5 4 3 2 1

CONTENTS

CONTENTS

INTRODUCTION

There you are standing tall, hand on the tiller of your beautiful sailboat. Gorgeous sunset, gentle waves, warm breeze on your face. Life is perfect. Until you get hit by a freak storm. In seconds, the sails are torn, the panicked crew is on the verge of mutiny, and your magnificent boat is sinking.

Now what? How do you react? What is your response to the chaos? Is it time to give up? Is it time to complain, blame others, or maybe jump ship yourself? Perhaps a few rounds of second-guessing are in order. Or simply grumbling about your 'bad luck' as you sit soaking and sulking on the deck.

For resilient leaders, none of the above is the correct response. Despite the circumstance, it is infinitely better to grab a bucket, bail some water, and hang on until the storm passes.

Stressful Storms

We all face storms, but why are some people able to carry on through them, while others are nearly destroyed? There are two factors at play: stress and the marvelous quality of resilience.

Simply put, stress is the mental, emotional, physical, and relational impact on people in highly demanding circumstances. Just how draining and destructive are these stress-storms? Here are some recent statistics to help us understand why resilience is so important:

- Over 60 percent of Americans say their stress level is at an all-time high.

- 55 percent of adults say they are unable to enjoy life due to the stress of personal finances/debt, mental health, physical health, home life, personal relationships, or job demands.

- Over 60 percent of adult Americans live paycheck to paycheck. That is approximately 200,000,000 people.

- Over 10 million Americans take medication for anxiety or depression.

- Approximately 20 percent of new businesses fail during the first two years.

Why do I share these troubling statistics? To show that we are all doomed to crumble under the stress of today's world? Not at all. This is where resilience comes in. As we study the beauty of resilience, it will help to understand the following foundations.

RESILIENCE is the ability to experience stress, loss, and other hardships and then successfully return to one's original state.

Resilient leaders are known for three primary qualities:

1. They intentionally optimize vital aspects of their health, including physical, mental, emotional, relational, and spiritual, while they minimize overall stress.

2. They successfully manage the performance of others.

3. They pursue worthy goals with optimism.

The impact of an optimistic mindset cannot be overstated. Resilient individuals see the bright side of the darkest situations and keep moving forward. For example, one person with a more negative view of things may lament that 20 percent of new businesses fail in the initial two years, while another person with a more positive view may rejoice that 80 percent of new businesses succeed during that same period. While resilience grows from a positive perspective, it also requires the consistent application of certain principles that can be learned.

We all face storms, but resilient individuals find a way through them to reach their destination. Consider the example from Cole Brauer who, at 29, became the first American woman to sail around the globe solo. During her 30,000-mile journey, she braved savage storms of hurricane-force winds and 30-foot waves. At one point, she was injured and had to give herself intravenous fluids. Mid-voyage, she single-handedly repaired her boat's failing navigational system. Truly, she is the epitome of resilience.

Like Ms. Brauer, we can employ specific strategies to avoid the temptation to head for calmer waters, and stay on course to achieve our God-given, world-changing purpose.

Team Success Starts With a Resilient Leader

It is common for leadership books to focus on techniques to include, inspire, and manage the performance of team members. While these concepts describe the purpose of leadership, they often assume that every leader who steps into the role is already rock solid, impervious to pain, and able to sail through any storm with bright smiles. As nice as that sounds, the reality is that leaders are only human, subject to the same stresses, problems, and storms as any other. Yes, we must develop our teams; however, a strong team starts with a healthy, resilient leader.

Resilience Requires a Reason

In this book, you will learn ways to significantly increase your resilience. However, I challenge you to determine the *reason* for your increased resilience. Its purpose must never be to help you simply endure an unfulfilled life, a dead end job, or any other form of drudgery.

Instead, the goal of increased resilience is to succeed where you are, building new strength and skills, and then push out farther from shore. Resilient individuals don't accept the status quo; they don't settle for less than the best, they refuse to lead lives of mediocrity. Chances are good that you can discover more, achieve more, and even love more than you can currently imagine. Be open to new possibilities, new doors, new vital relationships, new levels of influence, and new challenges as you move forward in life. Increased resilience helps ensure that you never have to settle for less than the best in any area of your life, be it personal or professional.

In the pages that follow, we will explore vital keys to resilience and hear from some amazing leaders who have been there, done that, and lived to talk about it.

Together, let's learn strategies to keep us sailing through the tempests that we are sure to face. When seas are calm, anyone can be a great sailor. However, true resilience can only be seen during and after the storm.

Storms are coming. Let's get ready...

CHAPTER 1

BUILDING A RESILIENT LEADER

S ooner or later, we all face tough times. These may come in the form of financial loss, relational breakdown, damage to our physical or emotional health, passing of loved ones, and many others. When these afflictions strike, we have two fundamental choices: we can accept them as natural parts of life's journey and keep going, or we can mumble, stumble, and finally crumble, unable or unwilling to carry on.

When counseling leaders in crisis, I often use the analogy that the tallest trees in the forest are the ones that face the strongest wind. In other words, leadership comes with unique types of resistance, pain and even suffering, that non-leaders never have to deal with. For resilient leaders, these setbacks are only temporary detours, not permanent stops.

Our resiliency does not depend on the severity of the hardship, but rather on how deliberate and effective our response to it is. Resiliency is much more than simply enduring. High-resiliency leaders not only survive, but thrive *because of* the trials, challenges, and setbacks that they have experienced.

Why It Matters

The concept of resilience is very personal for me. Early in my career, I burned out in a big way. As the founder and CEO of a growing consultancy, I approached my work as I did much of my life—full speed ahead. Stress was no big deal to me; I easily handled hiring and managing new professional staff, being a "good" husband and father to four young children, traveling the world to solve other people's problems, writing books, producing television programs, and more. I survived many days with only a few hours of sleep, and my usual breakfast was black coffee—no time for all that eggs and bacon nonsense. Lunch was a distraction, unless it was with a client. By two in the afternoon, I would start drinking caffeinated soda, continuing until late in the day, trying vainly to keep my energy level up. Life was a kaleidoscope of rental cars, hotels, and air travel. I hate to admit that the staff at several airline counters knew me by name. That should have been a hint.

My wake-up call came in Houston, Texas as two of my associates and I were preparing to give a presentation to a company headquartered in France. There was more than a million dollars' worth of contracts at stake, but to secure them, I had to hit a home run with my presentation to the group of decision makers, including some who had flown in from Paris. On the morning of the presentation, I woke up exhausted and dragged myself down to the hotel restaurant. As usual, I ordered coffee and began to slug down half a pot or so, just to start my engine. As I was getting ready to head back to my room to prepare for the presentation, a member of the client's leadership team entered, saw me, and sat down for a "brief" chat. Stress really kicked in as the brief chat turned into an hour-long conversation…and I was neither properly dressed nor adequately prepared for the presentation that was about to begin.

Finally excusing myself, I raced up to my room, threw on my clothes, and sprinted back down to the conference room, trying to look composed for the audience of decision makers. I made it through my initial presentation and retreated to my room to try to calm down. Unfortunately, my body was shutting down, and I felt terrible. My heart was racing, my head pounding, I had clammy skin and chest tightness… I was experiencing all the signs of a heart attack. I let my associates know that they had to cover for me for the remainder of the day. Then I grabbed my carry-on bag, hailed a taxi, and headed straight for the nearest hospital.

I spent the next three days in their Cardiac Care Intensive Care Unit, hooked up to beeping machines, downing nitro pills, and wondering what in the world had just happened. Finally, a very wise doctor came in and, much to my surprise, explained that my heart was fine. He then asked me a few questions about my lifestyle. As I shared my crazy schedule, lousy diet, physical inactivity, and everything else, he smiled and said "You are living with too much stress. You dodged a bullet this time, but if you don't make some changes, there might not be a next time."

Simply put, I had lost my resilience and could no longer bounce back. I confess that it took several months of laying low, resting up, changing my diet, exercising, saying 'no' to opportunities, and reconnecting with my family before I began to feel normal again. It took more than a year after that before I was back at full strength, willing and able to chase after worthy goals with a much more deliberate schedule and lifestyle.

By the way, we got the contracts. Whew…

Are Resilient Leaders Born or Made?

So, what causes one person to overcome challenges and another to falter? Is it natural ability? Charisma? A winning personality? Genetics? Phase of the moon? Perhaps it is something else.

In my seminars, I often ask the attendees whether they believe that resilient leaders are made or born. It does not take long before they reach the consensus that resilient leaders are *made* by their responses to life's challenges. This is great news, whether you are a professional athlete, single mother, or newly hired operator in a manufacturing plant. Resilience isn't about genetics, geography, or genealogy. We all start at the bottom rung of the resilience ladder and start climbing from there.

Qualities of Resilient Leaders

After working with countless leaders on several continents, I have reached the conclusion that the qualities which build resilience and those which diminish it are opposites. Based on many years of study, here is my list:

Resilient vs. Non-Resilient Leaders

- Stress Under Control vs. Stress Out of Control
- Purpose/Vision vs. Aimless/Short-Sightedness
- Balance/Pace vs. Workaholism
- Optimistic vs. Pessimistic
- Self-Control vs. Self-Indulgence
- Strategic Focus vs. Micromanaging
- Crucial Connections vs. Distance
- Self-Care vs. Self-Neglect/Self-Harm
- Faith vs. Fear

- Organized vs. Disorganized/Distracted
- Courage vs. Timidity
- Integrity vs. Hypocrisy
- Confidence vs. Self-Doubt
- Steadfast vs. Unreliable

On the pages that follow, we will investigate these marvelous qualities and see how they generate resilience. A small improvement in any of these qualities will make a difference. Small improvements in all of them will be life-changing.

POINTS TO PONDER

1. Have you ever been hit by an unexpected storm at work, home, or in your personal life?
2. What was the impact of that storm?
3. How did you respond?

CHAPTER 2

STRESS
CONTROL

AVOIDING THE PATH
OF LEAST *RESILIENCE*

ncreased resilience often begins with an overall reduction of stress. This is especially true for leaders. Why? Because higher levels of authority generally require us to support those around us in a variety of ways. Leaders must guide, supervise, provide resources, solve problems, listen to concerns and complaints, show compassion, make decisions, formulate plans, and develop contingencies for the plans that did not work—just to list a few.

Of course, the stressors don't stop at the end of the workday.

The business leader supervising hundreds of employees may also have responsibilities as a spouse and parent of children, young or old. He or she is likely responsible for a host of other duties, including some household chores, home maintenance, closet cleaning, and lawncare. The final layer of stress comes in the form of personal or inner conflicts as the need for 'free time' screams out for attention. So, how do we handle all this stress?

Stress management starts with an analysis of one's physical, mental, emotional, spiritual, and/or professional health. This is followed by the development of a plan to optimize each area. A common response to the call to reduce stress is "I don't have time." The pace of leadership often eliminates healthy activities such as rest, recreation, exercise, and quiet time with friends and family. It is true that a busy schedule may hinder opportunities to take care of personal health, such as medical checkups, counseling sessions, enough sleep, and more. However, these are all excuses, not valid reasons. When running as fast as possible, it is easy to forget that leadership is a long-distance race…without a finish line. If we don't manage our stress along the way, we minimize our effectiveness and can shorten our lives. This is no exaggeration.

I recently met with a group of physicians, nurses, and executives from a rural healthcare system. The meeting was chaired by the organization's CEO, who did a masterful job of leading discussions, resolving differences, and ultimately helping the group reach a consensus on some very divisive issues.

When the meeting ended, the room cleared, leaving the CEO and me to process what had happened. Unexpectedly, this marvelous leader dropped her head into her hands and closed her eyes. Concerned, I asked if she was alright. Her response amazed me. "I just can't get it all done…I am exhausted, but I can't let anyone know."

For the next hour, we talked about her life. She confessed the crushing weight of trying to be a good mother to two young teenagers, a good partner to her husband of twenty years, the leader of hundreds of employees, and the primary peacekeeper between feuding members of her medical staff, all the while trying to carve out time to do what she really wanted to do: have a day off to read a book, then take a nap.

This CEO is certainly not alone in her battle against the stresses of life and the isolation that often comes with leadership. I've known many leaders who suffer in silence, putting on a good show for staff, spouses and shareholders alike, while barely holding on themselves. The self-delusion is the belief that "if I just keep working long enough and hard enough, then everything will fall into place."

Here are a few facts that help us see a bigger picture when it comes to the impact of stress:

- Each year, over 765 million vacation days go unused by Americans laboring under the delusion that they are "indispensable."

- The average person gets less than seven hours of sleep every night, as opposed to the recommended eight hours or more.

- 50 to 70 million adults in the U. S. are affected by a sleep disorder and the percentage of adults using sleeping pills has more than doubled since 2010.

In the world of manufacturing, there is a concept called "preventive maintenance." This is the practice of shutting down a piece of equipment *before* it breaks from the stress of overuse. Every aspect of the machine is then inspected, oiled, greased, refitted, so that it is ready to function at a high level when it starts up again.

At first, this concept was criticized by those who quoted the common phrase, "if it ain't broke, don't fix it." Fortunately, the wisdom of preventing equipment problems is now the industry standard. Unfortunately, human beings are slow to adapt the same principle for themselves. Taking time away from the grind to focus on healthy habits seems like a waste, but in the long run it can prevent heart attacks, strokes, broken relationships, and general burnout. It is *well* worth it.

The approach to balancing work and the rest of life certainly varies between cultures and nations. In some cultures, including America, work can become all about position, possessions, and power. Bigger is always better. This approach is typified in the quip attributed to multimillionaire, Malcolm Forbes: "he who dies with the most toys wins." This flawed approach to life will eventually disappoint even the most dedicated climber of the corporate ladder.

In sharp contrast, other cultures see work as a part of life, but certainly not the most important part. For example, many Europeans use work to underwrite other priorities such as family, friends, hobbies, and personal interests.

There is a Bible passage that says, "What good will it be for someone to gain the whole world, yet forfeit their soul?" Modified for the modern world of work, this might read "What good will it be for someone to gain the promotion, yet forfeit their family, friends and health?"

The Real World of Stress

I've learned that the higher one's position of responsibility, the harder it is to reduce stress. This is true of high-level executives, midlevel managers, and single parents trying to succeed in their work, home, and personal lives. In these positions, there are simply not many natural opportunities for preventive maintenance on our minds, souls, and bodies. So, we must deliberately and strategically take time away from the crowd to rest, prayerfully seek direction, and simply shut out the noise, or else pay the price.

Excess stress may lead to emotional problems, such as depression and feelings of hopelessness. Some years ago, I was coaching an executive at a well-known Fortune 500 company. During our weekly sessions, he talked about the weight of his many responsibilities at work and at home. Over time, it became clear that he was experiencing an emotional freefall and was beginning to feel that his contributions had little value. One day, I sat across from him at a huge cherrywood table in the boardroom of his corporate headquarters. Dressed sharply in an immaculate blue suit, he placed his "lunch" (a huge 24-ounce plastic cup filled with caffeinated iced tea) on the table and slumped in his seat. The dejected look on his face spoke volumes about his emotional state.

"What's going on?" I asked him.

"What I do here just doesn't matter," he responded. "There are thousands of employees and hundreds of leaders. If I died today, I wouldn't be missed."

I sat quietly, knowing he had more to say. He then removed the thin plastic top from the massive cup and dipped his index finger into his tea.

"See? It's like the cup is this organization and my contributions are like my finger. Watch what happens when I pull it out…nothing. It's like I was never even here. I'm just wasting my time."

I confess that his demonstration shocked me. He was clearly losing the battle with stress. I considered how I might change his view, at least temporarily. I reached across the table, grabbed his cup, and poked a hole near the bottom with my ink pen. The iced tea began spurting onto the expensive table.

Instantly, he placed his index finger over the hole, stopping the flow.

"What are you doing?!" he yelled.

"Yours was a great analogy," I said, "but you missed an important point. The cup is your organization and the finger…the one stopping the mess from getting worse, is you. You have faithfully served here for years and solved many problems. You are extremely valuable as a leader and the company would lose a great deal if you weren't part of it."

I am happy to say that the impromptu demonstration took hold, and he began to smile. From that day on, we spent our time planning ways to reduce his stress, to increase time spent with family, as well as to make changes in diet and physical activity so that he could regain control of his life.

INTERVIEW WITH A RESILIENT LEADER:

MARILYN SKROCKI

Saginaw Valley State University

Position: Professor and Graduate Coordinator of the Master of Science Health Administration and Leadership at Saginaw Valley State University.

Professional: Fellow American College of Healthcare Executives (FACHE), Juris Doctorate in Master Business Administration and Master of Information Systems

Personal: Married to a role model leader, Don. Four children: Lindsey, Chad, Kristen, and Kristal.

What was your first leadership role?

My first leadership role was that of Risk Manager at St. Mary's of Michigan, an Ascension Hospital.

What did you learn from those early experiences?

That I needed to completely understand my role and anticipate future roles. I also learned that I put too much emphasis on IQ instead of EQ.

The most challenging part of leadership is:

Overcoming a fear of failure. Being supportive of my employees. Being assertive but not arrogant. Understanding there are always at least two sides to a story. Listening is more important than talking.

What are the habits or practices that help you remain positive, engaged, effective, and resilient?

Be curious and ask questions. Ask what if...? Remember to not take criticism from someone you wouldn't go to for advice. Experience has taught me that nothing is out of reach if you are willing to put a vision in place and start the hard work of achieving goals.

Describe a tough time that you endured as a leader.

I was downsized (along with the entire executive council) when a new CEO was hired. All the C-Suite executives were asked to either resign or take a lower position. I decided to leave the role of VP of Legal Affairs and pursue academia. I found I loved being in academia and it never felt like work.

How did it impact you and/or those around you?

I took a large pay cut, but my life and passion came back and that resulted in better relationships with my family and friends.

How did you overcome that tough time?

Pouring myself into my new role in academia helped me to focus on something else. I told myself, in this role, I would be able to either negatively or positively affect someone early in their career. Thinking of helping form opinions on careers was very humbling and I took it very seriously.

As a leader, did you ever feel like giving up?

Not really giving up, but wondering if I should go down a different tributary on the river of my career.

How did you overcome that feeling?

Always asking questions to those in careers that appeared interesting.

How has your leadership made a difference in the lives of others?

My hope is that my leadership is that of servant leadership. I often say Tim McGraw's song "Humble and Kind" is lyrics for leadership. I do what I can to help the next one in line. I hope that is how my leadership has made a difference in the lives of others.

Can you talk about an individual or a situation that helped you realize that you were making a positive difference as a leader?

My proudest leadership accomplishment is being a mom. When I look at my children, I see their curiosity about the world, their willingness to take calculated risks, their appreciation of education and their high emotional intelligence. To me, I believe my weird way of being a mom, with all the mistakes I made along the way, is my acknowledgement I must have done something right. In my professional career, receiving handwritten thank you notes, being in the grocery store and having a former student coming up to me to excitingly share where they are now in their careers makes me believe I made a positive difference as a leader.

Do you consider resilience to be more physical, emotional, or a combination of both?

I believe resilience is more emotional. If your mind is telling you not to try something because you might fail, resilience is silencing that voice and moving forward knowing you just might achieve it. Staying resilient is always seeing the glass half full instead of half empty.

What advice do you have for individuals in positions of leadership to help them stand strong during times of adversity?

Maintain your integrity. Adversity will come and changes will happen to your career plans, but if you falter in your own internal ethics barometer, you might be able to jump over a small hurdle, but you won't win the race.

MARYLIN'S KEYS TO RESILIENCY

1. Address and overcome a fear of failure.

2. Never take criticism from someone you wouldn't go to for advice.

3. Remain positive in the face of adversity.

4. What specifically will you do in response to what you just read in this interview? Set a goal.

CHAPTER 3

PURPOSE
IT'S *WHY* THAT MATTERS

There are few things in life that we do without a "why" attached to it. *Why* do we eat? Because we are hungry. *Why* do we sleep? Because we are tired. Why do we enter into close relationships? Because we want to love and be loved. We often say that something was done "on purpose," but a better interpretation is that there was purpose *in* what was done. For leaders, our work is satisfying only when we find purpose in the pursuit. Resilient leaders pursue worthy goals.

It is purpose that drives us, especially when we take on challenging tasks such as launching a new company or taking the helm of an existing one that is struggling to survive. Without a strong sense of *why* we are willing to work hard, sacrifice, endure opposition, and risk failure, it is likely that we will falter and fail. The good news is a sense of purpose or knowing why something matters provides strength, motivation and resilience when times are hard.

The need for clear purpose is shared by all leaders regardless of their scope of responsibility. The head of a multinational corporation oversees thousands of employees, while the leader of a corner coffee shop manages just a handful of workers, but both must know why he or she is willing to face the pressures that come with the role.

While responsibilities vary from leader to leader, the need for resilience does not. The impact of a failing CEO may extend farther than that of a budding entrepreneur, but consider the difference this way: if a multinational corporation's bottom line falls ten percent, the executives likely must do some restructuring. When a start-up coffee shop's bottom line falls ten percent, however, it could mean bankruptcy and financial ruin for the entrepreneur and family. Each of these leaders feels stress. Each must find ways to deal with the challenges. Each must understand his or her *why*.

Why does the struggling single parent rise each day to work jobs that barely keep food on the table? That's easy. The children need him. *Why* does the founder of a small company return to work just weeks after suffering a heart attack? That's easy. The employees need her.

I saw this in my own life many years ago, when stress and an unforgiving work schedule led to a burnout. During that period, the absolute last thing I wanted to do was get back on a plane or stand in front of a group of people in a seminar. All I really wanted to do was lie on the couch. Why did I get up? That's easy. My employees, clients, and family needed me.

Whether we describe our *why* as our purpose or our calling, each of us is motivated by something beyond ourselves. For some, it's all about bigger, better, and more. Others find purpose in building for future generations. For others, motivation comes from their vital relationships with family and friends, a healthy lifestyle, peace of mind, and the joy that comes from balance. It's all about the *why*.

What's Your Purpose?

Some years ago, Rick Warren wrote *The Purpose Driven Life*, which sold over 30 million copies and was translated into some 85 languages. Suddenly, people all over the world were trying to discover their purpose. Good news!

The bad news is that in the process, many discounted what they were currently doing and became discouraged by their lack of an official title or position. This was especially hard on stay-at-home parents who spent their days raising the next generation. Sadly, they failed to see the beauty of that role.

I think a better way to bring clarity to the issue of purpose is to ask yourself one simple question about your life: "What is the point?"

In other words, when you look at your personal life, your relationships or your vocation, determine how your life and the lives of those you care about are positively impacted by what you are doing. If you are in an entry-level position that pays your bills and you are learning principles of business, professionalism, work standards, and more, then it is easy to see the point in continuing down that path until a better door opens. However, if you are in an entry-level position that *doesn't* pay sufficiently to cover your monthly expenses; if you are in a role that pays the bills, but is personally unfulfilling, and there doesn't appear to be any chance for advancement; it is time to ask yourself that question: "Why am I doing this? What's the point?"

Keep in mind that this question should never lead to personal discouragement. Instead, it should be used to jumpstart careful planning for the next stage in your life where your next-level purpose will be found.

So, it's your turn. Why are you here on earth? What gifts do you have to share with the world? Are you currently living a fulfilling life of purpose, challenge, and appropriate reward? This is important—for you, those you love, and the world around you. Are you living your best life? If not, it's time to rediscover your purpose and not quit until you walk confidently in it.

POINTS TO PONDER

1. Do you feel fulfilled by your work? Explain.

2. What are some words that describe your purpose in life? What is important to you?

3. Which items are on your bucket list?

4. What specifically will you do in response to what you just read in this chapter? Set a goal.

INTERVIEW WITH A RESILIENT LEADER:
GENE PICKELMAN

Saginaw, Michigan, USA

Position: Founder, President, and CEO of Tri-Star Trust Bank founded in November 2000

Professional: Senior VP and Senior Trust Officer for Citizens Bank in Flint, MI responsible for the wealth management (trust) division southwest MI. Second National Bank (Citizens) for twenty-two years. Currently, Tri-Star has four locations; fifty-six employees and manages over $2. 3 billion in assets.

Personal: Married to Lori with two grown children.

What was your first leadership role?

I was branch manager for Second National Bank in Bay City, Michigan. I had the opportunity to start a new location after spending 1. 5 years in management training and being an assistant branch manager. I managed three employees.

What did you learn from those early experiences?

I learned that I had a lot to learn about leadership and managing people. If I'm honest, I treated people as functions rather than people. I was insensitive to their needs and more concerned about the success of the branch.

The most challenging part of leadership is:

To give up yourself. Once you give up yourself you can pour into people to help them be the best version of themselves. Took me several years to understand this. Humility goes a long way in leading others.

What are the habits or practices that help you remain positive, engaged, effective, and resilient?

1. Being focused on your purpose in life. This gives you direction and a sense of meaning.

2. Be present. Meet with your people consistently and engage with them. You cannot build a genuine relationship unless you engage with them.

3. Listen to your people and develop them. Provide technical, leadership and people skills training, and give them experiences at work that other firms would not offer. By investing in them, their loyalty to you and the firm grows.

Describe a tough time that you endured as a leader.

I co-founded a trust bank in 2000 with a business partner. I truly believed we both wanted to serve our clients in a caring and professional way. However, we had different ideas on how to deliver. This tension between us impacted the overall culture and our relationships with employees. It became so intense, the board had to get involved and define our roles going forward.

Tremendous leadership from the board who could understand this situation and look for a win, win, win outcome was crucial.

How did you overcome that tough time?

How I coped with this was to focus on the truth, live our values and show grace and compassion. I must admit that this was hard, and I failed many times. I focused on doing the right things and not worrying about the results. By the grace of God, we did endure and persevered and our business has been blessed. I also had great mentors in my life to speak truth to me and encourage me. This truly saved me and gave me the focus I needed.

As a leader, did you ever feel like giving up?

Yes. After four years of negative bottom lines and four capital calls, a stressed relationship with a business partner and slow growth during a recession, I really questioned if this was where I was supposed to serve.

How did you overcome that feeling?

First, I had to live out our business's higher purpose to "build genuine, caring relationships to strengthen families and transform community." People watch your behavior more than the things you say. Second, I realized that your staff make you successful and the best thing for me to do was to train and develop them. This became the secret to our success. Train and develop your people and you will retain them and attract new talent. Our employee engagement is over 80 percent and our client retention is at 99 percent. These stats show how our culture of caring for each other really pays off.

How has your leadership made a difference in the lives of others?

I made it a practice to take all new employees out to lunch after they spend 3-6 months with our firm. One day I took Lance out to lunch, and I was extremely moved by what I heard from him. Lance came to us from a competitor, working in the same position. He said, prior to Tri-Star, he would get up early in the morning, get ready, and leave for work before his family would get up. He would work 10-12 hours, come home, and had no energy for his wife and two children. Their relationships were breaking down, and he and his wife were discussing divorce. He shared with me that now he wakes up in the morning, gets ready and helps his kids brush their teeth, serves them breakfast, and helps his wife get them ready for school. He now comes home after 8 hours and has plenty of time and energy to pour into his family. They are no longer talking about divorce. So, what was the difference? Our culture. He said everyone was so nice and made him feel comfortable and needed. Did the prior company or his boss realize how their culture impacted his family? Did they care? Leaders are responsible for their culture and the health of relationships.

Do you consider resilience to be more physical, emotional, or a combination of both?

Both. To endure and persevere requires energy. When you take care of yourself, you are in a better position to succeed and remain focused. Determination and commitment require emotional strength—the ability to cope mentally. Being content with who you are provides a solid emotional foundation.

What advice do you have for individuals in positions of leadership to help them stand strong during times of adversity?

Three things:

- Wherever your foundation is, trust it. For me, it is my faith in God, along with living my values.

- Be honest with yourself. Focus on the truth and have the courage to do the right thing.

- Connect with mentors that will help you through—people you trust. Sometimes, especially with me, I miss the obvious. I need others to help me see the picture more clearly.

This is all easier said than done…but it can be done.

GENE'S KEYS TO RESILIENCY

1. Trust YOUR foundations in life: faith, family, friends, etc.

2. Build trusting relationships with those around you.

3. Find a mentor and listen to him or her, especially during tough times.

4. What specifically will you do in response to what you just read in this interview? Set a goal.

CHAPTER 4

BEAUTIFUL BALANCE & PROPER PACE

The Boston Marathon, the world's oldest annual footrace, was first held in 1897. Unlike today's modern event, which has more than 30,000 entries annually, there were only fifteen original runners who gathered at Metcalf's Mill in Ashland to run the 24.5 miles to Irvington Oval in Boston. The winner was Mr. John J. McDermott, because he understood the most important factor in the race: the proper pace.

We could learn a lot from Mr. McDermott's example and apply it to our work lives. Often, we approach our work as if it is a sprint, not the marathon that it truly is. First thing in the morning, the bell sounds, and off we dash. No time for breaks or an actual lunch—we just keep running until…until what? Until five o'clock? Six? Seven-thirty? For many, the workday is followed by a quick commute home, where we offer a hasty hello to family members, slam down dinner, and then jump back on the laptop to check "just a few" emails. Through bloodshot eyes, we grind until forced to seek the solace of sleep, only to restart the race a few hours later, fueled by the breakfast of today's corporate champions—namely, caffeine.

There is a huge problem with this approach. When it comes to our work, there is no finish line and, if you aren't careful, your pace becomes that of a sprinter, not a marathoner. There are no trophies, no medals, and no cheering crowds. These days, most organizations won't even offer a gold watch at the end of our race as a memento for years of toil. So why the rush? Why not set a pace that allows us to balance our work, relationships, and personal health? Why rush toward an uncertain end, leaving us with a trail of strained or broken relationships with loved ones, estranged from our children, and in ill health?

Resilient leaders must learn the lessons of balance and pace the easy way or the hard way. They either listen to those whose lives are beautifully balanced and properly paced, or they suffer loss of some sort before finally achieving harmonious lives.

Granted, there are times when we must put in extra effort and longer hours to meet a specific deadline. That's often part of the job. However, when one deadline bleeds into the next and then the next, then the "one-time special" deadline becomes a way of life. In this mode, there is no such thing as being *done;* you never catch up, and balance becomes an impossible dream.

Mastering the Marathon

While our work lives may resemble those of marathon runners like Mr. McDermott, there are two major differences. The first is found in training. Serious long-distance specialists spend years focusing on proper nutrition, stretching, running intervals, resting, insightful coaching, and practice, practice, practice. Contrast that with the "training" that some individuals have before being thrust into stressful positions of leadership. The high-performing worker is promoted to a supervisory position with the stroke of a pen, solely because he made the most widgets on his shift. The university graduate who spent years enjoying the good life at college is hired to "lead" a team of techies, and quickly learns how unprepared he truly is.

Many who step into positions of leadership have no idea the amount of work it takes to succeed. Their initial excitement and dedication keep them running, but without proper pacing, they soon struggle, as do their direct reports. At this stage, these rookies forgo any attempt at balance and try the guaranteed-to-fail solution of working harder, working longer hours, and ignoring signs of relational, social, emotional, physical, and mental disintegration.

The second major difference between professional runners and the rest of us lies in the intervals between big events. If, by some chance, there was another marathon race scheduled for the day following Mr. McDermott's big win, I guarantee that he would not have entered. Instead, he would have been resting, applying liniment to his aching legs, hydrating, and savoring his victory. Pace is important.

In many countries, men and women become so consumed with their work that they neglect other important areas of life. Family, health, joy, and peace of mind are sacrificed on the altar of one more year, one more deal, one more pay raise, and one more...whatever. When approached in this manner, the job becomes one's identity and the sole focus of life. In other words, we not only identify with our work, but our work becomes our identity.

Eventually, this comes to a screeching halt due to a health problem, downsizing, or some other cause for retirement. Once released from the arduous rat race, it seems logical that a person would enter a new era of health, but statistics show otherwise.

A study by Maria Fitzpatrick of Cornell University and Timothy Moore of the University of Melbourne found a significant increase in men dying at the age of 62. This is significant in light of the fact that the overall life expectancy in the US is just under 80. I'm no expert in this field, but I believe that the practice of living for work, running hard with no stops, and then experiencing the sudden loss of a work-based identity activates a host of negative behaviors and thought patterns that contribute to this growing phenomenon.

Many of these "end" problems could be prevented if we follow the advice of best-selling author, Dr. Stephen R. Covey, who encourages us to "begin with the end in mind." This "end in mind" thinking may be applied to either a short-term project or to life itself. Whether you want to build a house for the family dog or launch a multi-million-dollar product line, you need to clarify what the outcome should look like in order to determine how to balance and pace yourself along the way. This is true in countless areas of life. Enrolling in a university without first establishing an ultimate career path will likely waste a great deal of time and money. Entering a new relationship without a shared vision of where it's going may leave one or more individuals with a broken heart. Similarly, viewing your work as the end instead of the means to a better life can provide short-term satisfaction, but puts your overall legacy at risk.

Much thought is required to sort out the options and consequences of different paths, but it is well worth it. We have all regretted some impulse purchase, but we can overcome the loss of that $19.99, plus tax. However, we can't afford to live a life of impulse and imbalance, so we must think about the long-term impact of our decisions.

As leaders, we are not our work. Our work is not our identity. There is work, and there is life. So, if we want to live a long and satisfying life, we need to figure out ways to enjoy the journey rather than sprint till we stumble, tumble, and crumble at the "end." I am certain there was a wonderful celebration when Mr. McDermott crossed the finish line way back in the late 1800s. But every step, every meter, and every mile that John ran were milestones marking the way to his ultimate prize and each of them, no matter how small, was worth celebrating.

Here's how I learned to overcome this finish-line paradigm and build additional capacity for resilience. Instead of seeing life and work as one long race, ending in either retirement or my demise, I think in terms of well-paced segments or goals, then celebrate them along the way. Rather than measuring success at the year's end, or even quarterly, try looking at monthly, weekly, or even daily goals. Meeting or exceeding those goals then becomes cause for mini celebrations—an evening without thinking about work, for instance, or a full weekend of relaxation before diving back in.

POINTS TO PONDER

1. Are you in balance or out of balance in your life today? What should you change?

2. Have you set mile markers for your work and life so you can pace yourself along the way?

3. When you do pass a mile marker, how will you celebrate?

4. What specifically will you do in response to what you just read in this chapter? Set a goal.

INTERVIEW WITH A RESILIENT LEADER:

KEN HORN

Frankenmuth, Michigan, USA

Position: Executive Vice President of Strategic Development at the Great Lakes Bay Regional Alliance.

Professional: Former Michigan State Senator and current Executive Vice President of Strategic Development at the Great Lakes Bay Regional Alliance. In my current role, my work focuses on Operation 40K, an initiative I created to grow our region by 40,000 people by the year 2040.

In my former role, I was chair of the Senate Economic Development Committee, the budget subcommittee on Labor and Economic Opportunity, and the higher education Capital Outlay committee. In this role,

I also acted as chair of the Council of State Governments Midwest Conference, which included eleven states and four Canadian provinces.

Previous owner of a local restaurant.

Personal: Married to Veronica. We have two children, Kevin and Andrea. We have three grandchildren, two who currently live with us, Liam and Aaliyah, and Zellie who died in 2015.

* * *

What was your first leadership role?

My first true leadership experience was in the Frankenmuth Jaycees, where I won a Director of the Year award. I learned early on to watch and learn from others, then learn from my own mistakes in a supportive environment.

What did you learn from those early experiences?

Being a loner, asking for help was always, and still is, a hard thing to do. In the Jaycees, I was forced to ask for help as part of the projects we were all engaged in. Later in life, I had to ask because of the size of the scope of work I was involved in.

What are the habits or practices that help you remain positive, engaged, effective, and resilient?

Two things that probably seem unrelated; I never leave the house with the bed unmade, and I pray. The bed-making part is an act of self-discipline. I get up at least two hours before I leave the house for work, no matter what time I must leave. It all gives me time to unclutter my mind.

I pray for wisdom. I ask for eyes to see and ears to hear. Bishop Ken Unter used to say, "Every criticism, no matter how harsh, will always come with a grain of truth." Our staff would train constantly, me included, to ignore harsh language on the phone or in emails, to search for that grain of truth from constituents who contacted us with problems. When we got down to the bottom of their concerns, they were often surprised we were listening. They appreciated our help, even at the times we couldn't solve the problem they called on.

Describe a tough time that you endured as a leader.

The toughest time I endured as a human being, by far, was when I lost my granddaughter in a tragic accident. I was in the Senate at the time. It affected everyone around me. It changed who I was and how I viewed other people, including those I constantly butting heads with. I became more patient, less judgmental.

My most challenging time as a *leader* might be when I almost lost my restaurant business at the same time I almost lost my wife. Veronica got very sick in 1995 and went through a few surgeries. I became Mr. Mom, never missing a cupcake social at elementary school.

I became Veronica's caretaker as well and spent little time at the business. We estimate we were about a month away from bankruptcy before we, through sheer will, turned things around again.

How did you overcome that tough time?

I gathered my staff, told them the truth about the situation we were in, promised to work my tail off to bring customers back. And to prove to them I was serious, I woke up at 4:30 am every day, seven days a week for two years. I'd work until the kitchen closed every night, but still break away long enough to read to my kids before I tucked them in for bed.

People would ask, "how's business?" "It couldn't be better," was always the positive answer. That positivity seemed disingenuous at first, but it started catching on. We were all having fun, and the customers noticed it. In that first year, and every year after until I sold the place, we were hitting double-digit increases in food sales.

We went from eight employees to twenty-five and were even offering limited employer-paid healthcare at the end. After over twenty years, I'm still friends with the staff members who stuck it out with us.

As a leader, did you ever feel like giving up?

Hell yes, I felt like giving up. Lots of times. I couldn't afford to, though. I couldn't afford to be sick, and I couldn't afford to quit, financially, or morally. What kind of example would that have been to my kids?

After all, all the money I was supposed to make on the business was to pay for their college tuition one day. I couldn't let them down. I couldn't let my hardworking staff down. I couldn't let myself down.

How has your leadership made a difference in the lives of others?

This is a hard question to answer. I hope I've made a positive difference in the world around me. As for the lives of the people God graciously put into my life? If I've failed them by the advice I've given, or the examples I've set, I hope they can forgive me.

But when they succeed in life, I know it's because of *their* hard work and *their* persistence, not mine. And I'm proud of them all.

Can you talk about an individual or a situation that helped you realize that you were making a positive difference as a leader?

Leading in economic development, and in my last years in elected office, I'd have industry and community leaders come to my Capitol office saying they'd been directed my way by my colleagues from both sides of the aisle.

Today, I can point to the Hudson Tower in Detroit, for instance, and say with confidence, "I'm not a steelworker or a carpenter, but I helped build that building." It surely would not have been built without the legislation I wrote. It took a team and great patience and persistence to get that Brownfield Transformational Act over the finish line.

In the last week of my final term, our Senate Majority Leader gifted each of the members of his leadership team with a beautiful leather laptop carry case. The Majority Leader and I had a rocky start, but in the end, my leather case was engraved with the term, 'Senate Majority Leader Consigliere.' Because I never lied to him, he trusted me with some of his most important and most difficult leadership decisions.

Do you consider resilience to be more physical, emotional, or a combination of both?

Both, but mostly emotional. Working twelve to twenty hours a day is one thing, but emotion can cause stress. And stress can have a physical effect, too. Everything is connected to everything when a person is facing heavy and constant pressure.

To relieve stress in my life, I worked out physically. I started training and teaching martial arts early in owning my business. It wasn't long after I went through the toughest time at the restaurant that I went into a six-month intense training program for my black belt.

People should know both aspects as they seek their own work/life balance.

What advice do you have for individuals in positions of leadership to help them stand strong during times of adversity?

Know yourself, be honest with yourself. Know your strengths and weaknesses, and don't be shy about surrounding yourself with people who fill your gaps.

For example, I know I'm a creative person. I solve problems. I make connections for people. I'm bad at organizing and filing paperwork. I hire people to overcome my flaws. I help people solve problems and my team makes sure those problems stay solved as I go on to the next one.

When you find that right person, or people in your life, whether it be a spouse, chief of staff, or partner in business, make sure they aren't 'yes' people. Surround yourself with loyal people you can trust (and be trustworthy yourself) and listen to them when they disagree with you.

KEN'S KEYS TO RESILIENCY

1. Be honest with yourself about strengths and weaknesses.

2. Find *your* way to relieve stress.

3. Develop self-discipline and stay consistent with good habits.

4. What specifically will you do in response to what you just read in this interview? Set a goal.

CHAPTER 5

OPTIMISM

Why do some see the glass half full, others half empty, and yet others fail to see the glass at all? In a word—perspective. We will invariably face storms in our lives. The variable is *how* we face them, so a choice must be made between a positive or negative outlook.

There is an old English proverb that says, "You may find the worst enemy or best friend in yourself." In other words, *you* are the one who determines your perspective and response to any situation. Some choose an immature response to challenges and waste time complaining, blaming others, and looking for the least painful ways to quit. A much more mature approach is to take responsibility for a solution, encourage others, and keep moving forward.

This professional approach takes courage and stamina, as well as mental toughness. Challenges can be hard, but negativity only makes them harder. This is especially true for a leader, whether in the workplace or at home. Both negativity and positivity are contagious, and leaders set the tone for everyone looking to them for direction in a storm.

The optimistic leader focuses on possibilities and options, thereby energizing, inspiring, and calling others to exchange their fears for productive action.

We all have encountered negative people, whether at work or in some other setting. You greet them with a hearty "good morning!" and their response is "what's so good about it?" This type of individual often moves from pessimism—believing that *their* life is horrible—to cynicism—trying to convince you that *your* life is horrible, too. Don't let them.

Optimists are not cluelessly stumbling around, wearing rose-colored glasses, oblivious to the troubles of life. They are quite the opposite. Keenly aware of surrounding circumstances, optimistic leaders spend their time deciding on the best ways to achieve their worthy goals despite the challenges. This approach results in high levels of resilience.

I love this quote from Benjamin Franklin: "While we may not be able to control all that happens to us, we can control what happens inside us."

Positive or Negative?

The contrast between positive and negative outlooks on life are universal and timeless. In the late 1800s, author A. A. Milne wrote a series of stories whose characters provide a brilliant contrast between optimistic and pessimistic perspectives. His main character is a bear named Winnie the Pooh, who glides through life with a smile and kind words for others. Another character is Eeyore, a donkey who gloomily wallows in mud, complaining, just waiting for the next bad thing to happen.

Perhaps some people are born with a personality that naturally makes them more like Winnie the Pooh than others, but for many, optimism develops with time, experience, and reflection. The minor disappointments of life don't cling to resilient people like they do to Eeyore. Instead, they serve as lessons learned and mile markers along the way to greater resilience.

Optimistic Leaders

Optimistic leaders know that despite setbacks, they and their teams will find ways to overcome the problems, right the wrongs, and keep moving forward. They have learned that complaining only demoralizes both the complainer and those that hear the negative comments, thereby reducing resilience.

For those in leadership, each day brings a host of new opportunities and challenges. In most cases, we get precious little prewarning for either one. Not long ago, I consulted with a struggling Midwest manufacturing company that wrestled with the increased costs of raw materials, new competitors, and low employee engagement. Throughout my time there, I marveled at the impact individual midlevel leaders had on their respective departments. The more positive leaders projected an upbeat can-do message as they increased their interaction with team members. They remained gracefully honest about the situation, but consistently explained reasons for hope, even as they identified areas where improvements could be made. Unfortunately, other managers went in the opposite direction by hiding in their offices, sending out gloomy emails about the problems faced, and threatening that if things "did not change," the company would be in deep trouble.

As you can imagine, the more optimistic leaders saw robust responses from their teams, who brainstormed multiple ways to save money, increase productivity, and improve the company's chance of success. In other parts of the organization, the pessimistic "leaders" saw little to no improvement, morale continued to lower, and the best team members left the organization.

In this organization, each department faced the same threats, the same possibility of job loss, and had the same resources to work with. The difference in performance was directly tied to the level of optimism in the leader and the approach used to motivate the staff. Resilient leaders instill resilience in those around them.

Opposites Attract?

Scientists have long known that opposite charges attract each other, and similar charges repel each other. They explain that, since electrons have a negative charge and protons have a positive charge, they are drawn together. This is also seen with magnets. It is impossible to put the same poles together, as the magnets push apart. However, if you put the opposing poles together, the magnets link together. A few more examples of opposites attracting are found in electrolysis and even in the clouds, when colliding particles result in thunder and lightning.

While this concept of opposites attracting is proven in science, it is not the same when it comes to leadership and the quality of resilience. Positive leaders do not attract negative team members, but often repel them. Why? Because positive leaders don't waste time complaining, listening to excuses, or enduring substandard performance. Now add in resilience, and the gulf between the positive and negative individuals gets even larger. A co-leader or team member lacking resilience turns away from the tempest, looking for a place to hide, complain and ultimately quit. A resilient leader turns into the storm to find a way to survive it and stay the course.

POINTS TO PONDER

1. Is your approach to life and leadership more positive or negative? Why?

2. What sort of team members do you normally attract?

3. Would those around you describe you as positive, negative or a combination of both?

4. What specifically will you do in response to what you just read in this chapter? Set a goal.

INTERVIEW WITH A RESILIENT LEADER:
KELLY LESEMAN

Anchorage, USA

Position: US Public Health Service Officer

Professional: My career has focused mostly on small communities and isolated rural villages which are mostly off the road system. I am an engineer and project manager by trade. Most of my work is with the native tribes, and small communities or villages. After graduating college, I worked for a private engineering firm for four years. I then served twenty-six years as a Commission Corp Officer in the US Public Health Service. I have been operating my own business as a private consultant since 2019.

Also, I serve as the Executive Director for Proyecto Fe, a non-profit ministry which supports education, healthcare, and a mountain ministry program in the Lake Atitlan of Guatemala. My love for volunteering and adventure has taken me to the jungles of South America, to the slums of Temor-Leste, and many places in-between.

Personal: I live in Anchorage, Alaska with my wife Wendy. Our two adult children live nearby.

* * *

What was your first leadership role?

My first experience was managing construction projects. This had two fronts which needed to be managed separately. First were our team members. The second was the village or the tribal leaderships we were working for. As an engineer, managing projects was not technically difficult, but what they don't teach you in engineering school is how to deal with or manage people. This was a steep learning curve. Fortunately, I was under good leadership myself and had good mentors to teach me.

The most challenging part of leadership is:

Knowing how to deal with people. For someone to want to follow you, they need to respect you. Respect is earned, not demanded, no matter what your position is in life. Respect is also a two-way street. Once you have mutual respect, it is much easier to provide leadership and discuss any differences which may come up in executing a plan.

Describe a tough time that you endured as a leader.

I brought the tough time on myself when, early in my career, I would put on my engineering inspector's hat and start pointing out all the things not in compliance with the design. My style was not leadership, it was dictatorship.

How did it impact you and/or those around you?

The work did not get done and the culture was toxic. We all suffered.

How did you overcome that tough time?

I changed my tactics. I'd show up to a job site, roll up my sleeves and help work. I'd ask them to teach me stuff like sweating pipes, installing pumps, or electrical panels. These projects were in small, remote, and isolated Alaskan villages, typically off the road system. There were no grocery stores, Costco's, or convivences we often take for granted. The crews had to live in these communities while they worked. So, I started bringing them fresh milk, steaks, and produce. I'd even cook dinner for them. Once I started dealing with the crew as people and earned their respect, they started looking for my leadership.

The other lesson I learned during that time was to never assume you know more than others do. Never dismiss someone's idea or suggestion point blank or put them down for suggesting something. Even if you know it's a bad idea or will not work. Help them work through the thought process and logic of their decisions and what the impact may be.

How has your leadership made a difference in the lives of others?

The eureka moment of leadership came in Koyuk, a small, isolated village in Norton Sound in Western Alaska. This village had no running water. Residents had to haul their own water and waste. We're talking third-world sanitation conditions. We built a complete water treatment and distribution system, wastewater collection system, plumbed homes and brought clean water to every home. About two weeks after we turned the tap on and people had running water, I was walking around the village. One of the tribal elders ran out of his house yelling, "Kelly, Kelly, come here!" He grabbed me by the arm, led me into his house, to the bathroom, and showed me his flushing toilet. This guy was in his 70s and never had running water or a flushing toilet in his life! He was so elated and grateful. This was the moment I quit thinking it was about me and realized it was about serving others, making a real and meaningful difference in people's lives.

The desire to serve others has done more for my leadership abilities than anything else. Leadership skills and abilities can be taught and learned. However, the desire to serve others can only come from the heart. When the two come together, when your leadership skills are fulfilling a higher purpose, God will use you beyond anything you could imagine.

Do you consider resilience to be more physical, emotional, or a combination of both?

It is both physical and emotional but probably more emotional. It is a mindset you must possess. A good similarity is what aircraft pilots call "situational awareness"—making a conscious effort to be aware of your surroundings, your environment, taking in the factors which may cause you to react, and having knowledge and skills to react accordingly when needed.

What advice do you have for individuals in positions of leadership to help them stand strong during times of adversity?

Managing your team and human resources is probably the biggest challenge when facing adversity. It's much easier to be a leader when everything is going well. It's when things do not go well and facing adversity where true leadership is tested. Just look at Covid and the negative impact it had. This was a true test of leadership for many of us. True leaders keep their teams engaged in developing and executing solutions.

Early in my career I learned a valuable lesson. When things go wrong, don't worry about who caused the problem. Instead, put your efforts into finding a solution. A good leader doesn't play the blame game when faced with adversity. They engage their team and find solutions.

KELLY'S KEYS TO RESILIENCY

1. Engage those around you when looking for solutions.

2. Focus on serving others, rather than being served.

3. Understand the situation before you react.

4. What specifically will you do in response to what you just read in this interview? Set a goal.

CHAPTER 6

SELF-CONTROL
NO THYSELF

Socrates, the ancient Athenian philosopher, famously said, "To *know thyself* is the beginning of wisdom." By "know," I am sure that he meant to understand one's abilities, limitations, weaknesses, and strengths—all great things to "know" for those in leadership today.

However, I want to add the following twist to Mr. Socrates' saying: "*NO* thyself." By this, I mean that among all the other important things a leader must know, he must learn when to say "no."

Why is this tiny little word so important for those in leadership? Because leaders are constantly under pressure to perform, to attend meetings, to meet deadlines, to coach others, to be, to do, to go, and more. The human body, brain, and emotions simply are not designed to function under this sort of pressure day in and day out.

Face it, leadership is intoxicating because of all the perks. These may include higher compensation, good benefit packages, office space, windows, company car, bonuses, etc., as well as the power to hire, fire, and promote others. Once tasted, it is hard to let go of these benefits, even for leaders who are in danger of ruining their health, their vital relationships, or their long-term legacy. There is another aspect of leadership that often prevents letting go or at least slowing the pace of the ascent to higher heights—namely, the roar of the crowd. I confess that, in the months leading up to my burnout, I fell into this seductive trap. At that time, I was solving the problems of multiple companies on multiple continents, while negotiating long-term contracts at others. In addition, I was writing books and making television appearances. The pace was grueling, but the applause and money and new opportunities kept coming, so it never made sense to tell myself to slow down. Meanwhile, no one else was going to help me toss out my anchor because, if you are performing at a high level, the beneficiaries of your hard work certainly won't tell you to stop. It's in their best interest for you to keep going.

When we are headed toward the top, it is counter-intuitive to do anything that might slow our ascent. Yet it is the perfect time to take stock of what truly matters. Your family, your values, your health, your long-term legacy, your *why*. Upon reflection, you may find that you need to need to cut back or to make a change that allows you to live in a way that is true to yourself and to what matters to you the most. That is what I did, eventually, and thank God it wasn't too late.

Today, many know the reasons why they do what they do. I have a friend who gave up a high position within an institution so that he could work with youth in his community who desperately needed a wise mentor. Those around him thought that he was crazy to give away so much, and yet, my friend never hesitated, walking away from a position of power and local fame to pour into the next generation. Simply put, my friend said *no* to himself, and *yes* to his higher purpose. He found his *why*.

POINTS TO PONDER

1. Do you find it difficult to say 'no'? Why or why not?

2. If you often overcommit, why do you think that is?

3. What are some strategies to help you balance your time?

4. What specifically will you do in response to what you just read in this chapter? Set a goal.

INTERVIEW WITH A RESILIENT LEADER:

CARL JEFFREY WRIGHT

Chicago, Illinois, USA

Position: CEO of Urban Ministries, Inc.

Professional: I serve as CEO and President of UMI (Urban Ministries, Inc.) a position I have held since 1994. Before that, I served nearly twenty years in Fortune 50 healthcare companies in a variety of leadership positions. My last position was Vice President of Business Development for Bristol Myers Squibb's global consumer business. I have been in positions of leadership for over forty years.

Personal: I live and work in Chicago, Illinois. Married to Lakita and have four children: Stephen, Amanda, Natalie, and Justin.

* * *

Describe your organization.

UMI is a fifty-three-year-old publishing and media company with a product line of curriculums, magazines, books, and digital media primarily used in African American churches nationally with some limited product distribution and donations made globally, but primarily in Africa. Throughout its history, UMI has served over 40,000 churches and millions of consumers with bible study resources and other Christian education content.

What was your first leadership role?

My first leadership role was student body president as a college senior. I was a young senior at nineteen years old and I quickly learned that, as a leader, I could not please everyone who looked to me for direction and influence. The clerical workers at my college sought me out for student support in a wage increase action where they wanted me to lead and support them with a student strike or protest. The administration reached out to me, and they made the case that the increase the workers sought would inevitably require tuition increases. It was a dilemma that put me at odds with my constituents, the students, the workers we sympathized with, and the administration who showed me the books and made a compelling case.

What did you learn from those early experiences?

The leadership lesson was simple: you can almost never make everybody happy.

The most challenging part of leadership is:

Maintaining consistency in attitude, demeanor, practices, and relationships.

As a leader, what are the habits or practices that help you remain positive, engaged, effective, and resilient?

I depend on my faith, which includes practices of prayer and meditation, scripture reading and study, private and public worship, along with wisdom from other leaders to keep a positive attitude and to make certain that I do not easily fall for negative outlooks or emotions. Also, I am a voracious reader and I constantly seek new ideas, information, and strategic insights that will inform my leadership.

My goal is to develop deep relationships with the people I lead, and I always try to make sure the teams I lead feel supported by me in their entire lives and not just their life at work.

These spiritual practices also remind me that the privilege of leadership is the privilege of serving others. If I can help people perform their best and get results by the support, encouragement, and effective problem solving in areas that I alone can do as a leader, the results are usually effective and resilient leadership.

Describe a tough time that you endured as a leader. What happened?

The Covid crisis was a tremendously tough time for me as a leader because the shutdown affected churches and we sell products to churches. We lost nearly half our sales in less than twelve months, requiring cost cuts and layoffs as well as creativity in trying to survive as an organization in a tough market environment that required new solutions for survival. During this same period, I was diagnosed with cancer and, just a few months after that, the founder and chairman of my company passed away. This series of crises and losses had a tremendous personal impact on me, but I was able to contain much of my own fear, uncertainty, and doubt so that I could be an encourager for my team. In the end we came out smaller but stronger and more efficient as a company. I am now a cancer survivor, and our organization is on a solid path to recovery and growth.

How did you overcome that tough time?

By continuing and even increasing my practice of more disciplined prayer and by recognizing the great

privileges we all have as people in the US, the richest
and most powerful nation in the history of the world at
this time, I was able to keep the losses and health challenges in perspective. Despite all that we went through,
we were still blessed to have the resources and external
environmental support that come from simply being in
America.

As a leader, did you ever feel like giving up? How did you overcome that feeling?

I have felt like giving up many times. I have not given
up though because I understand the gift and the
opportunity that leadership has afforded me. I don't
mean pay or perks but rather the opportunity to be
used by God to bring excellent products and support to
our customers. If we do great work, we help churches
do great work and that is a good thing. All of us have
an assigned part in bringing these Kingdom outcomes
and, when I view them as my central assignment and
not ancillary to my desires and interest in fun, food,
family pleasures, and funds in my bank account, I am
immediately sobered up with the reality that there is
only one way off the planet and, when it happens, I will

be held accountable, as we all will be, with how we did on our assigned work. That gets me out of pity parties and back to work every time.

How has your leadership made a difference in the lives of others?

I hope I have helped others find meaning and purpose in deeper and richer and more fulfilling ways through my leadership. I have cared for people and their families in ways that I believe have made a difference in their daily lives. I have always tried to reward people with pay and benefits that exceed the work environments they have experienced in the past. I ask people to bring their best leadership practices from their past employers to our company so we can implement them if possible. That has led to several innovations and new practices from other people's experiences. Sometimes these have been small but meaningful improvements, like a massage chair in the employee break room. In other instances, there have been more long-term impacts, like a continuing education program that has paid for degrees that actually led to people leaving us for new work experiences.

Can you talk about an individual or a situation that helped you realize that you were making a positive difference as a leader?

We often have the experience of hearing from our customers—pastors, teachers, students, parents, and others—who let us know that the products we create have made a positive difference. I have also seen growth in several individuals who started with us with high school or undergraduate college education only and ended up with PhDs and significant leadership roles in much larger organizations with greater social and global impact.

Do you consider resilience to be more physical, emotional, or a combination of both?

Whenever an "either-or" choice is presented, there is almost always a "both-and" answer. Our physical condition affects our emotional condition, and the opposite is also true. This has been determined by medicine and science, and we neglect either our physical or emotional health and well-being at great risk to our overall health. A leader needs to take care of spirit, body, and mind.

What advice do you have for individuals in positions of leadership to help them stand strong during times of adversity?

Know what you believe and believe what you know. If you are a person of faith, you should be ready to defend your faith and clearly express why you believe what you believe. The power of faith has stood the test of time and circumstances through adversity. Just trust and obey!

CARL'S KEYS TO RESILIENCY

1. Live *your* beliefs in all situations.

2. Practice spiritual disciplines.

3. Never quit. Regroup and pursue your vision.

4. What specifically will you do in response to what you just read in this interview? Set a goal.

CHAPTER 7

STICK WITH STRATEGY

Imagine a pitched battle between two medieval armies. On the front lines, combatants take turns attacking and defending, hoping to gain an advantage. The opposing kings are there in the muck and mire, showing a willingness to sacrifice for the cause. There is one downside to this approach, however: the leaders are so consumed with the urgency of the moment's tactics that they have no time for strategy. Under these circumstances, *if* the battle is won, it will be by blind luck rather than design.

Over time, the role of leaders on a battlefield changed. Now, military leaders remove themselves from the noise and chaos of the frontlines, so that they can have a fuller view of the situation. From this vantage point, they can:

- Have time to think, plan and respond.

- Prepare the best strategies to protect those under their care.

- Decide on proper utilization of resources.

- Leave tactics to those best suited to the task.

Very few of us will ever lead troops in combat, but we can learn valuable lessons from those who have. Unlike the kings of old and their time spent shoulder to shoulder with the troops, there are no "honor points" bestowed on supervisors, managers, or executives who linger long on the front lines. In fact, those that do are classified as "micromanagers"—hardly a desirable title. This doomed approach erodes the resilience of a leader as he tries to balance overseeing fine details of a work process with accomplishing his own higher-level tasks.

There is a delicate balance between the roles of leaders and of their followers. When leadership fails to provide proper strategic direction, the team's performance grinds to a halt. It is not the job of direct reports to develop comprehensive strategies so, without clear direction, many staff members simply do what they did yesterday, even if it isn't what needs to be done today. At the opposite end of the spectrum, there are leaders who feel the need to micromanage even the smallest tasks, thereby abandoning the high ground. Just like the kings of old who rode into battle without a concrete plan for their troops, this is a sure way to lose resiliency.

When a leader micromanages others, it results in one of two scenarios:

1. Direct reports hate it…because they want to do their work. This creates resentment on their part, and they ultimately shift into neutral gear while their leader flails around in unfamiliar areas.

2. Direct reports love it…because the leader is doing their work for them.

However, there is one important reason for higher level leaders to *temporarily* come down to the trenches: in order to clearly understand what front-line staff are dealing with. Strategic leaders must know:

- What challenges are the troops facing?
- Do they have sufficient resources to accomplish desired tasks?
- Are they trained adequately to succeed?
- Are they properly rested, motivated, and engaged?
- Are mid-level leaders effective and encouraging?

Armed with this information, top leaders then head back to the high ground, where they develop strategies, distribute resources, and craft communications to keep the rest of the team informed as well as inspired.

Successful leaders are those who trust those working under their care and, instead of spending time in the trenches counting widgets, they spend it on the high ground, developing long-term strategies to overcome the opposition. This approach prevents burn out and helps develop resiliency in the team and the leader alike.

POINTS TO PONDER

1. Could you be accurately described as a "control freak" or micromanager?

2. If so, how does this impact your resilience?

3. How can you better balance your need to know and the need to let others do what they must do?

4. What specifically will you do in response to what you just read in this chapter? Set a goal.

INTERVIEW WITH A RESILIENT LEADER:

TREVOR JOHN KNOESEN

Port Elizabeth, South Africa

Position: Founder and CEO of Productivity Improvement Consulting Company

Professional: I worked as an Industrial Engineer with 3M South Africa and later moved to Anglo Dutch for another two years to manage their Industrial Engineering, Production Planning and Control, and Warehousing. Prior to launching my own firm, I worked as Senior Project for the Manager South African National Productivity Institute (NPI). I worked for the NPI for thirteen years and was awarded the highest consistent achiever before leaving.

Major projects have been concluded with Delta Motor Corporation (formally General Motors), VW of South Africa, Daimler Chrysler of South Africa, and Toyota South Africa. Through our work at VW, we were invited to undertake projects in Brazil and Poland.

Personal: Married to Maria Magdalena Knoesen for forty-nine years. Have two children: Dean and Shiree. We have four grandchildren: Ava, Ben, Charlotte, and Emily.

* * *

What was your first leadership role?

I served in the Rhodesian Territorial Army and spent nearly five years in combat. I was eventually promoted to Acting Platoon Commander.

What did you learn from those early experiences?

In my early role of leading troops in combat, my objective was to develop a closely knit team that would rise to any occasion based on loyalty and respect for one another. A team that cared and looked out for each other. A team that was united, like a family. You had to know each other's strengths and weaknesses; in fact, you had to know everything about each other. This way, comradery excelled through the good and most difficult times. When a command was given, everyone trusted and worked as a unit, to firstly survive and secondly to be victorious. There were times when the wrong strategy was adopted, but we triumphed in every circumstance as we operated as one in unity.

The most challenging part of leadership is:

To gain the confidence and respect of those who work for you. To achieve this, you need a close bond. When we face challenges, we open everything up in discussion. We identify the problems and then each gets their chance to voice a solution or way forward. I listen because my managers are often at the coalface more than I. If their solution is better than mine, I adopt their solution. However, there are often traps and experiences they have not seen in their careers, that I have encountered, and I convey these to the situations we face. In cases like these, I will make the final call and there is enough respect, though they may differ in opinion, that they genuinely follow through with what I have decided. I am very careful to give them all the credit for every successful project. We succeed and fall with each other.

As a leader, what are the habits or practices that help you remain positive, engaged, effective, and resilient?

I think the main attribute to remaining positive is my faith in God and knowing this is the path He chose for me. In addition, I do believe He gave me a long apprenticeship in being a successful productivity consultant. Most projects or contracts are well within my "personal wheelhouse" and, for whatever other reason, I have always been very confident that I/we can deliver. There are bumps in the road at times, but these are "normally" relatively easy to overcome by working as a team.

Describe a tough time that you endured as a leader. What happened? How did it impact you and/or those around you?

In my forty-two years of consulting, I/we have only had one failure. I secured a good contract with a company, after I had found there were serious productivity issues. The main problem was that one of the directors, who controlled the operational arm of the company with an iron fist, did not fully understand how to optimally manage his plant. The Managing Director of the company (whose Head Office was in another location in the country) suspected that his plant was not performing well operationally. I pointed out that, should we be awarded the contract, we would never succeed if this director remained on site. The Managing Director arranged that he be given an overseas assignment for the time it would take for us to complete the contract. Everything progressed very well until his loyalists were secretly reporting our progress to him overseas. This was going to embarrass him, and he created circumstances to return urgently. On his return, those loyal or intimidated by him literally sabotaged successful improvements already made and were in progress. He then convinced the Managing Director not to pay us our final contractual amount due at the end of the project.

As this was going on, I instructed my team to complete the assignment in the best possible way under trying circumstances, while I tried to counter the problem. This was not of the team's making and they could only control their own work performance. The added incentive to keep maintaining their motivation was that they were not carrying the heat and I was guaranteeing them they would not be financially disadvantaged in any way. The final outcome was not a great one and I lost a fair amount of money, but none of my people lost any income. The upside of this debacle was the resultant additional goodwill and loyalty from my team, knowing that I placed their best interests above profit.

How did you overcome that tough time?

It was difficult, to say the least, and I carried a high level of personal stress. With it being a sizeable project, the financial loss hurt a great deal. In addition, I had to undertake damage control within a group of companies we worked with, that related in a value chain program to his company. In consulting, reputation is everything.

A hundred great projects go by relatively unnoticed; encounter problems on one and it can come back to bite you badly. Very fortunately, I had a good relationship with the Managing Directors within the other value chain companies, and they reported that they were having their own problems with the same director that had caused me all the trouble.

As a leader, did you ever feel like giving up? How did you overcome that feeling?

This may seem insincere, but the honest answer is, no. It's a profession I understand well and have been exceptionally successful at. There have, however, been numerous times over the years when I faced very stressful times. These occurred when there were gaps between projects and contracts. My modus operandi was to always keep my core managers, even if there was no income, as if I let them go, we could never undertake the larger projects and contracts, which always tended to surface. Managing cash flow and reserves was difficult and I confess I did get despondent at times.

How has your leadership made a difference in the lives of others?

I think this has been well-covered already. Often, when a subcontract consultant decided to leave, they would personally come to see me resigning. In virtually every case, they would have preferred to stay, but as I could not offer permanent employment, they had to consider more stable employment for the sake of their families. The theme was always that no employer would have ever done as much, over and above the terms of agreements set. Some said they felt that leaving was like a divorce, because they all felt part of the family we created. Through the experience they gained, many of these young men have developed and fast forwarded their careers. Some of my managers that left have since created their own consulting businesses. It is a dilemma that I have always accepted, in that one is training up potential opposition. However, the net result and "good feel" is that I have developed people that have benefited considerably in their profession and enhanced the welfare of their families. The other advantage is that we have all remained great friends.

Can you talk about an individual or a situation that helped you realize that you were making a positive difference as a leader?

There was one occasion when a situation on a project had the potential of getting out of hand and the Managing Director had severely criticized one of my managers. He was upset and could not see a way forward. Fortunately, he came straight to me. We dissected what had transpired and why. His logic on the course he was following appeared correct to me. There was a technical issue overriding some bottleneck machinery in a chain of a production sequences, which he had taken verbatim on information from shop floor supervision. If we could prove this information, it would vindicate him and prove to the Managing Director that he was correct. I called on an expert mechanical engineer I knew quite well, and the net result was that my manager had in fact determined the process capability and capacity correctly. We both went to the Managing Director and very diplomatically placed the evidence before him. He was thrilled and it lifted the spirits of my manager and enhanced his reputation with the Managing Director.

Do you consider resilience to be more physical, emotional, or a combination of both?

It's a combination of both. Resilience starts with initial negative emotion, then once the dilemma has been examined, problem-solving is developed, which leads to alternate solutions, and positive emotion emerges. This follows action and, after solving the dilemma, it finalizes the road of resilience.

What advice do you have for individuals in positions of leadership to help them stand strong during times of adversity?

While self-confidence to overcome is a critical ingredient, it is important in times of adversity to rally relevant expertise, and close confidants, mostly close trusted colleagues, and even friends. Determine what alternatives there are to get through the adversity presented and listen to others. In other words, "take council." If one is a faith-based person, also consult trusted spiritual leadership as well as praying in a way that you believe God will bring you through the storm. At times, the clearest answer comes this way.

TREVOR'S KEYS TO RESILIENCY

1. Remain confident during times of testing.

2. Stand up for yourself and your work when challenged.

3. When a solution is needed, involve others that may see things different from you.

4. What specifically will you do in response to what you just read in this interview? Set a goal.

CHAPTER 8

CRUCIAL CONNECTIONS COUNT

There is an undeniable connection between a leader's resiliency and his or her team's performance. An under-performing team is a source of stress for both the organization and its leader. Time spent checking and rechecking progress, fixing mistakes, and refereeing interpersonal conflicts lowers a leader's resilience. Similarly, a productive team suffers when its leader has low resilience, because his or her dearth affects the team members in the form of negativity, lack of creativity, and an overreliance on rules rather than on productive relationships. The ideal leader-team relationship is one of symbiosis, whereby each benefits the other in many ways.

The key to optimizing the benefits of this relationship is a leader's bond with those who serve under his or her care. Even in today's world of remote work with staff members spread across the globe, leaders must still find ways to connect with team members or risk losing synergies and other benefits.

Even though leaders are extremely busy, they must be regularly seen and heard by those they supervise. This is not "drive-by" leadership, where the leader races through an area smiling and waving like a celebrity in a parade, or just sends out a weekly email update. Instead, leaders must set time aside to truly connect with, listen to, communicate with, instruct, and genuinely show compassion for the challenges of those whom they lead.

This requires a paradigm shift for those who mistakenly believe that their highest purpose is to hit certain numbers, achieve arbitrary milestones, or set new performance records. I'm convinced that leaders that chase numbers tend to lose their people. A better approach is for leaders to forge deep connections with team members, then inform, inspire, and properly resource the team so that *their team* hits the numbers, achieves the milestones, and sets new records together.

In a recent corporate seminar, I used the following phrase to describe this revised mindset: a leader's primary responsibility is to *"create the environment that allows his or her direct reports to succeed,"* even in the absence of the leader.

I then asked the attendees to write a list of the essential items that their direct reports needed to know in order to properly do their jobs. The results were fascinating. Some of the leaders listed job descriptions, others stated some of their unwritten expectations, still others used generic terms such as "work together, work smarter not harder, and show respect." Once the lists were completed, I asked a few more questions.

"How many of you have items on your list that could be misunderstood or misinterpreted by your employees?"

Every hand went up. Then, I asked them to do a very unscientific survey.

"Ideally, you've prepared 100 percent of your direct reports to understand 100 percent of their responsibilities, expectations, timelines, and priorities that you have set for them, right? So, look back at the list you just created, and rate how prepared your direct reports truly are today."

The room was somber as each leader reported back to the group. The most common preparedness rating was 70 percent, but some were as low as 20 percent. Obviously, these were subjective guesses, but the leaders were stunned to consider that those huge gaps translated into low performance for the team, and a less-than-stellar rating for the leaders themselves.

I had a few more questions.

"How will your direct reports grow in their abilities to perform, if that vital information doesn't come from you? And how can you provide the information if you don't spend time mentoring, encouraging, connecting with them?"

The obvious answer was, "they won't" and "I can't."

We then spent time creating strategies for the leaders to close the gap through increased connection, instruction, and a greater investment in the development of team members. The leaders realized that, once these strategies were implemented, they could then invest more of their energy into innovation and spend much less time putting out corporate fires.

I can guess what you are thinking. As a leader, you have no extra time for this connecting business. You are swamped as it is. Right? On the contrary, you don't have time *not* to connect with your team, because when direct reports lack essential information about timelines, standards, and priorities, their performance is low and they will ultimately be forced to reach out to someone to get the information piecemeal, and repeatedly. That someone is you, and the constant bombardment of questions, mistakes, revisions, and major messes depletes a leader's resilience. As the classic television ad for auto maintenance says, "You pay me now, or you pay me later." Better to make the investment in staff now.

I've worked with many leaders who struggle to leave the confines of their office to connect with their direct reports. Often, their reluctance comes in four categories:

1. The leader feels too busy doing other "important" things.

2. The leader is concerned that these interactions will turn into gripe sessions.

3. The leader does not know what to talk about.

4. In the worst cases, the leader feels "above" this practice, only wanting to interact with subordinates "when necessary."

My rebuttal for each is:

- **Too busy.** For leaders, there is nothing more important than staying connected with direct reports.

- **Fear of complaints.** There is always the possibility that discussions may turn into gripe sessions, and while that might be uncomfortable, it is not entirely bad. It's better to know what people are thinking so that issues can be addressed, than it is to wander around assuming that all is well when it isn't. If issues are raised respectfully, then leaders have nothing to fear and plenty to learn.

- **What to talk about.** Just ask about how a person's family is doing, how they plan to spend their weekend, or to share ways that they could be better supported at work.

- **Not worthy of your time.** If you feel like this is below you, you don't understand your role as a leader…You likely won't last long in your position.

This connected approach to leadership is more art than science, so there is no simple formula to follow each day. However, once the principle of connectedness has been embraced, then leaders can easily decide how to apply the principle. Here are a few examples:

At times, this may require a brief visit to a busy department or area to explain an important detail or new development. At other times, the leader may need to stop and calm agitated staff members along the way. Also, a watchful leader can spot "mentoring moments," whereby a staff member's performance or approach could be improved with a suggestion from the leader. On some occasions, leaders find it beneficial to set aside time to bring an entire group, department, or shift together to discuss new developments or other important aspects of the job.

Each group and individual may respond differently to a leader reaching out, especially if previous interactions were less than productive. A few direct reports might be intimidated or resentful, but the vast majority will be thrilled at this new approach to leadership. This is especially true during times of organizational stress, when a visit from the leader has a calming effect on the team. It is sad to say that, in some organizations, those at the top do the exact opposite, hiding in their offices as if waiting for the storm to pass and hoping that "those people out there" know what they are doing.

A deep connection between leaders and team members results in a very powerful bi-directional loyalty. Whether you call it sowing and reaping, karma, or the law of reciprocity, staff members generally give back what they have received. In other words, when followers know they are being instructed, cared for, listened to, and sincerely communicated with, they often make deep commitments to both the leader and the overall organization. This is true whether in multinational corporations, new entrepreneurial enterprises, or even our homes.

POINTS TO PONDER

1. Which methods have you used to connect with those who work under your care?

2. What personal and family details do you know about those who work under your care?

3. How might a deeper connection between you and those who work under your care lead to greater resilience on your part?

4. What specifically will you do in response to what you just read in this chapter? Set a goal.

INTERVIEW WITH A RESILIENT LEADER:

DR. DAVID J. HOBBS

Lake City, Michigan, USA

Position: General surgeon

Professional: Twenty-four years from CMU Leadership Scholar to present career as a physician. I'm a surgeon that performs inpatient (emergent) surgery, elective out-patient surgery, and endoscopy, and I care for patients in the hospital and outpatient clinic, often taking regional call for northeastern Michigan.

Personal: Married to Kaitlin with five children, ages three to thirteen.

What was your first leadership role? What did you learn from those early experiences?

I served as a Worship Leader in my local church, overseeing volunteer musicians and technical people on my team. I learned that not everyone sees things the same, has equal commitment to a vision, and some will even work against others if they don't get to "steer the bus."

The most challenging part of leadership is:

Working alongside people who may have personal agendas or ulterior motives that don't seem to align with the purpose of the team.

As a leader, what are the habits or practices that help you remain positive, engaged, effective, and resilient?

Learning to adjust to the constant change can be difficult when you are in leadership, but it seems a whole lot easier when I am centered on my faith. When I keep myself (my previous plans, emotions, etc.) in check with this ideal mindset, I can remain functioning as a leader that is engaged and effectual. However, it can be difficult to demonstrate resiliency when your situation isn't unfolding as planned.

Describe a tough time that you endured as a leader. What happened? How did it impact you and/or those around you?

My toughest time happened just recently. I got caught in the middle of a situation where hospital administration tried to achieve the appearance of a perfect culture by addressing even the most minute complaints of staff members, even from those who were proven to be constant complainers. As a surgeon, the approach from Administration put me in an unwinnable position. During intense surgeries, if I didn't politely ask a subordinate, in just the right words and tone, to focus on the tasks at hand in order to save a patient's life, then the subordinate would file a written complaint with the administration. This meant hours of 'investigation' and then follow up meetings to confirm that I had not been 'too harsh,' etc. This approach literally put patients' lives at risk, so ultimately, I became exasperated with the system, and agreed to resign to pursue other options. Sadly, I had to sign a non-compete agreement which made it illegal for me to practice my profession within 100 miles of our home. Obviously, this put tremendous pressure on my wife, children, and me.

Truthfully, this situation has been terrible for me, and it still isn't completely resolved. Oddly, there are times it has been refreshing to see all the options open to me within other hospital systems, as well as starting my own practice. I confess that, at times, there is a fear that things could get worse before they get better, and I have to battle feelings of betrayal from the administrators that I faithfully served for years. One thing is sure: this upheaval is teaching my wife and kids to depend more on the faithfulness of a perfect God and less on me as a perfect father. I may fail, but He won't, and that's a good lesson!

How did you overcome that tough time?

This situation continues to unfold so I'm still in the process. I've positioned myself with more experienced leaders and mentors to seek their advice, and I've obtained legal counsel. I make sure that I am present for my family, in spite of the turmoil, and work hard to keep any bitterness from taking hold of my thinking.

As a leader, did you ever feel like giving up? How did you overcome that feeling?

Absolutely. There have been several times where I've wanted to throw in the towel, sell it all, and move on to an easier life in a different location. However, those feelings were very short-lived, and, in a sense, very transient. I love seeing God work on our behalf, and I believe that I'll see the goodness of God in my situation. I think that inner knowing of his providential goodness keeps me going—it is, in a sense, a co-laboring with Him that puts wind in my sails when I'm temporarily lacking the fortitude to keep going forward.

How has your leadership made a difference in the lives of others?

I find this challenging to know. Based upon my conversations with a diverse group of exceptional leaders, it can be difficult to sum up the difference you've made in the lives of others. We may not hear from everyone we have impacted or influenced, so who knows? When it happens, when you see the difference, it is wonderful. Earlier in life, I enjoyed and even sought out recognition, but that has changed a great deal now. I'd prefer to know that I did my best and let that speak for itself.

Can you talk about an individual or a situation that helped you realize that you were making a positive difference as a leader?

As a surgeon, I often meet people during their greatest time of need. Often, they are scared, confused, or both. I love the fact that I can talk with them before the surgery to help calm them, and then meet with them afterward and explain that it went well. Patients and their families often demonstrate a lot of gratitude for surgery.

Do you consider resilience to be more physical, emotional, or a combination of both?

Both. However, if I had to choose one, it would be emotional. It all starts on the inside with how we think and what we say during times of great stress.

After years of education and training in my field, I learned to handle the physical stresses of late hours, little sleep, and an unbalanced diet. By staying mentally strong, these things were just obstacles to be overcome versus showstoppers.

What advice do you have for individuals in positions of leadership to help them stand strong during times of adversity?

It's important to remember that we grow stronger in the fight. And we don't often actualize the strength and lessons learned from the prior fight until it repeats, perhaps with a slight twist. Now I apply lessons from previous fights in my present situation. God uses and wastes nothing in our lives.

DAVID'S KEYS TO RESILIENCY

1. Learn from previous battles and mistakes.

2. Remain committed to your faith foundation.

3. Let go of anger, bitterness and resentment, even when you have been mistreated.

4. What specifically will you do in response to what you just read in this interview? Set a goal.

CHAPTER 9

SELF-CARE

W ay back in 1976, the Kenner Company produced a toy that generated over $50 million dollars in sales. The toy? Stretch Armstrong, a ten-inch latex action figure, filled with corn syrup. What made this toy so successful? It stretched. Really far. As in, kids could grab an arm or a leg and pull old Stretch way out of shape. Once they let go, the limb would slowly regain its original shape, ready to be pulled in another direction again and again.

Stretch Armstrong remains the epitome of resilience and a wonderful model for those of us in leadership. No matter which direction he was pulled in or how bent out of shape he got, Mr. Armstrong always readied himself for the next tug.

As leaders, we get used to being pulled in many directions, and our acceptance of this lifestyle seems to grow with time. We tolerate the intolerable pattern, letting back-to-back meetings, a dozen text messages, a handful of "do you have a minute?" interruptions, two soccer games for the kids after work, and only a few hours of sleep become the norm...for a while. Humans were not created to endure years of constant stress; without proper adjustments, the results can be fatal. This is where self-care comes in.

Self-care is the practice of intentionally managing one's mental, emotional, physical, relational, and spiritual health. Why is it called *self*-care and not simply care? Unfortunately, it is because often there is no one else to ensure that leaders are well cared for.

Executives, managers, supervisors, administrators, parents, community officials, religious leaders, etc., are often the last to receive care from those they serve. After all, leaders, are supposed to have it all together, right? Not exactly. In my experience, the higher the position of leadership, the less likely that others will approach us with concerns about our wellbeing. Therefore, we just keep going, mistakenly thinking that things will somehow, some day, slow down. So, we put in an extra hour or two at work, make late night phone calls that take "just a few minutes," and practically mainline caffeine just to stay in the game. This pattern continues at home, as the lawn grows to look like a meadow, the family car needs repairs, the neighbors want to come over for drinks, soccer practice rides must be arranged, that medical checkup has been pushed off for six months, and there is no way to cram all of it into your day, or week, or month, or year.

The new badge of honor in the corporate world comes in the form of heart attacks, burnouts, breakdowns, and trips to rehab to get rid of bad habits caused by the stress. Remember, leaders usually can't count on someone else to passionately push them toward good health. They must rely on self-care.

Do you need more proof? Here are a few statistics and studies that are both interesting and disturbing.

When there is no self-care, we are prone to suffer from one or more of the following:

- Lack of sleep
- Anxiety
- Depression

- Distraction

- Irritability and anger

- Fatigue

- Low self-esteem

- Relationship dissatisfaction

- Lack of empathy and compassion for others

According to the Centers for Disease Control and Prevention, it's estimated that six out of ten Americans suffer from a chronic condition, and four of those ten suffer from two or more. These conditions include Type 2 diabetes, Alzheimer's, stroke, heart disease, cancer, chronic kidney disease and chronic lung disease. Hundreds of thousands of lives in recent years have been lost from opioid abuse, whether from prescriptions or illegal street drugs. About 88,000 people die of alcohol-related causes every year in the United States.

I'll stop there with the stats, studies, and sad stories. Suffice it to say, we have some work to do when it comes to our health.

So, what causes these maladies? I'm no doctor, but I work with many, and they tell me that the fundamental causes of most health problems are:

- Poor nutrition
- Excessive use of alcohol
- Insufficient exercise
- Tobacco use
- Lack of preventative care

The good news is that every item on this list is fixable. Each of us has the option of eating better, cutting back on alcohol, exercising, tossing out the smokes, and establishing healthy self-care habits that allow both sufficient freedom and proper restraint. It just has to start with motivation and a decision.

Many leaders unintentionally play a form of Russian roulette with their health. Nothing bad has happened (yet), so why not keep going? As someone who has fallen into this trap, I can tell you that it is far better to proactively address your health needs than to wait until you suffer a heart attack, like I did a decade ago. I assure you that, when you are being wheeled into the operating room for heart surgery, your thoughts are about your family, friends, and the beauty of life—not on some meeting, project, or deadline. Once I recovered, I made some simple adjustments to my physical activity, diet, and stress management, which not only saved, but changed my life.

Self-Care Strategies

There's more good news: those of us in leadership are not doomed to endure painful lives of chronic stress, sleepless nights, and pill-popping just to survive. We just need a comprehensive strategy of self-care. While this approach to life may not be easy, it can be simple. Cut back on the bad stuff, do more of the good. Get up and walk. Take the stairs. Get regular health checkups from a medical provider. Knock off the junk food. Get some sleep. Simple, but not easy.

About a year ago, one of my sons talked me into going to a local gym three days a week. Our workout involved lifting weights, stretching, and walking on the gym's padded track. I confess that this was a significant change from my normal "business mode," so the initial two weeks were challenging— by which I mean that I was barely able to move the following day. However, I persisted; after the first week, I realized that it was getting a bit easier, and my body was a little less sore. By the end of the second week, the soreness went completely away, and I began to notice increased strength and flexibility. By the end of the third week, I couldn't wait to get back there. Like that shoe ad from a couple years ago, we need to "just do it."

There are several categories of self-care to consider:

Physical Self-Care

This may be the easiest to monitor. It includes:

- Regular health checkups to identify and treat current problems as well as prevent future ones.

- Getting sufficient sleep (and shutting off your phone, social media, and other electronics early in the evening to promote good quality sleep)

- Establishing an exercise and activity routine that you can maintain

- Monitoring your alcohol intake

- Eating nutritious foods and a healthy, balanced diet (helps your body prevent, fight and recover from infections as well as impacting your mood)

Emotional and Mental Self-Care

Do things to help return balance to your heart and soul, and which serve as pleasant distractions from the pressures of life. These may include:

- Taking appropriate breaks from work
- Sharing your true thoughts with a trusted friend or counselor
- Going for walks outside
- Laughing
- Scheduling recreational activities that you enjoy (fishing, golf, hiking, etc.)
- Picking up a new hobby (painting, playing chess, studying ancestry, etc.)
- Reading books that you find interesting
- Learning a new skill or studying a foreign language

Spiritual Self-Care

It doesn't take many years on earth to realize that there are mysteries, miracles, and fascinating aspects of creation all around us. The answers to many of life's questions are more spiritual than they are physical or emotional. Spiritual self-care may involve:

- Attending worship services
- Personal prayer or meditation
- Counting blessings instead of problems
- Acts of kindness toward others
- Volunteering at a worthwhile community program
- Offering forgiveness to those who have wronged you

Resilience comes much easier when our whole being is healthy. We have a significant capacity for stretching but, unlike old Stretch Armstrong, if we don't implement strategies of self-care, then some aspect of life will lose its resilience—and then eventually break. Don't let that happen.

POINTS TO PONDER

1. What is your current approach to self-care?

2. Rate your approach to the following using *pass* or *fail*. Do you have. . .

   - Adequate rest and sleep

   - Proper nutrition

   - Physical activity

   - Supportive relationships

   - A trusted friend, mentor, or counselor to talk with

   - Regular medical check ups

3. Which of the above are you most concerned about?

INTERVIEW WITH A RESILIENT LEADER:

BETHANY ANN CHARLTON

Saginaw, Michigan, USA

Position: Chief Executive Officer of Covenant Health-care System

Professional: I have formerly been a Nurse Manager, Project Team Manager, IT Manager, Critical Care Director, Vice President of Patient Services, Chief Nursing Officer, Chief Operating Officer/Executive Vice President at Covenant HealthCare. I have held formal or titled positions of leadership for approximately thirty-five years.

Covenant HealthCare is a healthcare system in central and mid-Michigan and the Thumb. It has approximately 4700 employees and hundreds more physicians and volunteers providing care for approximately two million patient touches annually.

Personal: Married to Chris for thirty years and have three grown children: Nate, Nicole and Catherine.

* * *

What was your first leadership role?

I served as the Interim Nurse Manager for a Pediatric Intensive Care Unit.

What did you learn from those early experiences?

Leading people is a privilege and has very little to do with power but much to do with influence and impact on a collective whole. Also, people want to know how they are doing, how they are impacting the output, when they do well and how they might need improvement. I also learned that being a leader at times takes courage.

The most challenging part of leadership is:

...Also the best part of leading. It is a human-based intuition and skill set applied to individuals and groups; therefore, you never know what you are going to get!

As a leader, what are the habits or practices that help you remain positive, engaged, effective, and resilient?

Frequent reflections back to the mission. Opening meetings with "Moments that Matter," a story or highlight about things being accomplished. Participating in a "Code Honor"—going to a department to honor a vet upon their death—or talking with new employees in orientation to hear why they chose Covenant Health-Care when they could choose any other system to work. These interactions, along with work on active listening and reflection are my best and most effective builders of strength. Candidly, also reading and prayer.

Describe a tough time that you endured as a leader.

Leading Incident Command during the Covid crisis. Our community was hit pretty hard, and our hospital became a central care-giving entity for our state during that time. For a period (that felt endless), we had more inpatient care-giving demands than any other organization in the state of Michigan. We had many employees get seriously, even gravely ill, and two of our team members passed away.

How did it impact you and/or those around you?

We were tired, weary, and even angry or sad. We also were innovative, resilient, courageous, and creative. We employed humor and deeply relied on each other for strength and spirit boosting. I have never felt more a part of a *team* than during that time. We all had a common enemy.

How did you overcome that tough time?

The last part of my answer above. The team. Prompting collective efforts, having the courage to make a mistake, admit it, pivot, and move past it. Communication and more communication on the goal and how we were doing. Celebrating the "wins," big and small. Giving and receiving grace!

As a leader, did you ever feel like giving up? How did you overcome that feeling?

Of course, there were times that felt insurmountable, where I might, as an individual, have felt like it was "bigger than myself," but I didn't get to a place of giving up because the stakes were too high. Before I reached a breaking point, there were others around to lend strength so I could regroup. Hearing about accomplishments of our system's care was my strength. Care for the community, care for the team. That doesn't mean I didn't have emotional responses and even at times, broke down. For me, that time was in the car on the way home, away from others.

How has your leadership made a difference in the lives of others?

I have had people tell me that the way I accomplish my work and assert my influence has made a difference for them. In caregiving, you often have the privilege of impacting something immediately, with everything from listening to actual intervention. Leadership is like that too, although often in the moment you do not get the immediate result or impact. It comes later or in a subtle way. I notice more of those outcomes now. The development of culture, the development of committed teams and team members, accolades and awards of acknowledgements, that simply are not possible without thoughtful and dedicated leadership. Since I have been a part of this team for thirty-five years, I would humbly say that I have made a difference.

Can you talk about an individual or a situation that helped you realize that you were making a positive difference as a leader?

Being at the helm during a worldwide pandemic and helping our organization to succeed was the pinnacle of my career.

Do you consider resilience to be more physical, emotional, or a combination of both?

Both, but if I had to state which is more necessary, I would say emotional fortitude is greater; without it, our physical self will not thrive in times of challenge.

What advice do you have for individuals in positions of leadership to help them stand strong during times of adversity?

Simple words: listen, know thy strengths, know thy weaknesses, have humility, and give and receive grace.

BETH'S KEYS TO RESILIENCY

1. Draw strength from others *before* you reach your breaking point.

2. Stay focused and committed to a process even if you don't see immediate results.

3. Let the people around you know how they are doing to keep them motivated.

4. What specifically will you do in response to what you just read in this interview? Set a goal.

CHAPTER 10

CONTAGIOUS FAITH

Our world is filled with contagious conditions, some good and some not so good. The common cold, influenza, and whooping cough may be transmitted to others, but so can yawning and laughter. There are two other aspects of the human condition which are highly contagious: fear and faith.

Fear is a distressing emotion caused by the presence or *anticipation* of danger. It is important for leaders to realize that fear is highly contagious, and it can occur even when there is no actual danger at hand. We live in a stress-filled society, and stress is taking a toll on us in many ways. According to the National Alliance on Mental Illness, over 40 million adults in the United States have some sort of anxiety disorder, and nearly 10 million are prescribed anti-anxiety medicine each year.

People worry about all sorts of issues, including money, health, career, relationships, appearances, world events, politics, and a host of others. Fear, anxiety, and worry are like waves that continually slap against the shore, washing away resilience, courage, and the will to continue to try. Because fear and anxiety are so prevalent, we must remember that our friends, family, or team members may be struggling with these as well. Thankfully, we have medical and mental health professionals that help people cope with their fears. In addition, we have another resource to counteract fear, which is just as contagious—faith.

Please don't take a too limited interpretation of the term. By faith, I mean the assurance that someone or something will bring about a good end to a situation. We may put faith in God, faith in our family members, and/or faith in ourselves.

When speaking to groups of leaders, I often ask an odd question: "How many of you consider yourself to be a 'big deal,' as in something special?"

Out of thousands, I've only seen a few hands raised. I don't think this is from a sense of false humility. Instead, I think the vast majority of those in leadership positions truly don't see themselves as anything special.

This sort of humility is a wonderful quality for those in leadership; however, any strength taken to extreme may become a weakness. In this case, it is extremely important for leaders to know that to their subordinates, they *are* something special. Here's why: organizational leaders are given tremendous power over the lives of others. When one can hire, transfer, promote, reward, and even dismiss others, he or she is viewed differently from coworkers, peers, or fellow team members. I often explain to leaders that their voices are louder, their actions are magnified, and that they are constantly being watched by those that work under their care.

So, what does this have to do with faith? Plenty. During times of uncertainty, change, or turmoil in particular, the words and actions of leaders set the tone for the rest of the organization. I've worked with leaders as they struggled with organizational, personal, or even existential problems, and was amazed to observe how the response from staff mirrored the actions of the leader. If leaders looked, acted, or sounded nervous, it sent shockwaves through the subordinates. Conversely, when leaders projected confidence and took the time to explain how the challenges could be overcome, the rest of the organization followed suit, went to work, and did what was needed to succeed.

Sometimes, a confident assertion that "it's going to be okay" from a faith-filled person is all it takes for others to calm down, refocus, and shape their future rather than dreading it.

Years ago, there was an ad for an antiperspirant that featured an NFL coach who showed the importance of leaders projecting confidence to those around them. He said, "*No matter what the score, never let 'em see you sweat. Everyone feels pressure. Winners don't let it show.*"

Leaders, whether in an organization or in a family, set the tone, the tempo, and the culture for everyone else. I call this "being in the fishbowl," as others constantly watch for verbal and nonverbal cues about the stability of the present and the security of the future.

Leaders that encourage others with confidence and an uplifting word leave an inspirational trail of faith about the future. Of course, this does not mean that a leader should lie or mislead others for the sake of positivity—this tactic would result in a loss of credibility.

Instead, when faced with challenges, it is healthy for leaders to communicate the basics of the situation with an optimistic "glass half-full" perspective. In brief, this is what needs to be explained to set troubled minds at ease:

1. Here is the storm we are facing.

2. Here is our strategy to weather the storm.

3. Together, we *will* get past this storm.

There are very few situations that threaten the existence of an organization, but a panicked or fearful group of staff can certainly create a self-fulfilling prophecy, driving things from bad to worse.

On the other hand, a leader's expressed faith in the future and confidence that all challenges can be overcome lifts the spirits of the team and helps keep them focused on the mission and values.

Keeping It Real

The pressures of leadership, whether in the marketplace or at home, often produce moments of doubt. We may question a decision we have made, wonder if we are headed in the right direction, or even wrestle with our own ability to make it all happen. Fear creeps in, doubt sneaks into our thinking, and, if we aren't careful, we start sliding down the slippery slope of catastrophic thinking. When—not if—that happens, it is the perfect time to toss out the anchor and examine our faith. Here's how I approach it:

- Do I have faith in my company's mission of helping organizations and individuals reach their fullest potential? Is it still valid? If the answer is yes, I keep going.

- Do I have faith in my family, that they are still supportive of my work and lifestyle? If the answer is yes, I keep going.

- Do I have faith in my coworkers, that they are committed to our mission and are faithfully living our values? If the answer is yes, I keep going.

- Do I have faith in myself, that I am committed to my mission and am living our values? If the answer is yes, I keep going.

- Finally, do I have faith in God and his direction, provision, and grace? If the answer is yes, I keep going.

With each "yes," my commitment grows, my energy is restored, and my resilience is assured.

In the interest of keeping it real, it is important to realize that there may be times in life when the answer to one or more of the above questions is actually "no." When that happens, it means that something significant has changed either in our work, family, connection to God, or within ourselves. When that happens, what is the best response? My recommendation is threefold:

1. First, pause and determine what changed. Did something traumatic happen? Has your team lost focus? Are there family issues that need attention? Has there been an unanswered prayer? Has compromise crept in to some area?

2. Second, once the area that needs attention has been identified, pause long enough to address it, even if that means that other aspects of life must be temporarily put on hold.

3. Third, make the tough decisions that will restore that wonderful sense of faith in your life. This may mean a return to your original worthy goals at work, making changes to your staff, or spending

additional time with family members to establish the bonds of supportive relationships.

If you find that you have lost faith in your own abilities, then seek counsel from wise people who care about you, so you can regain the true picture of your worth and contributions to the world around you. If you have lost faith in God, communication with a clergy member and some time spent in prayer may help reframe the marvelous connection between the Creator and his creation. Faith lost can be regained and restored.

POINTS TO PONDER

1. How does your leadership impact those working under you?

2. How do you feel about being in the "fishbowl," where others see and judge your performance?

3. What strengths do you bring to your workplace and, if applicable, to your home?

4. What specifically will you do in response to what you just read in this chapter? Set a goal.

INTERVIEW WITH A
RESILIENT LEADER:
JOEL A. FREEMAN

Baltimore, Maryland, USA

Position: President of The Freeman Institute

Professional: Served as mentor and chaplain for the NBA Washington Bullets/Wizards for twenty seasons. Cofounder of Black History 365®, an educational company that publishes educational curricula and resources for public, private, and home schools.

Personal: Married with four children: David, Jesse, Jacob (deceased), and Shari

What was your first leadership role? What did you learn from those early experiences?

Way before I launched into corporate work, I actually became a pastor after three years of Bible School training. We sent out mission teams from the Baltimore church to Puerto Rico and to the Dominican Republic.

I learned that loving people right where they were at was important. Studying to be a good teacher was equally important. And being a consistent person— always on time and a man of my word—were hallmarks of how I chose to live my life.

The most challenging part of leadership is:

Consistency. Life hands us all of the highs and lows. It is important for a leader to be the shock-absorber for others. It's tough being consistent, especially when the leader is going through a low time, feeling used up, or burned out.

As a leader, what are the habits or practices that help you remain positive, engaged, effective, and resilient?

One of my nightly practices is to prepare for the next day the evening before by keeping short accounts with God in prayer regarding the day's activities. I liken this prayer to an Olympic runner who has dug in, preparing for the pistol shot. Hence, I am preparing myself for the first moment of consciousness at the crack of dawn.

Describe a tough time that you endured as a leader. What happened? How did it impact you and/or those around you?

It's far too personal to put in a book because of the people involved, so I'll just say that being betrayed by others created my toughest times in life.

How did you overcome that tough time?

Refusing, with gritted teeth sometimes, to take revenge. Forgiving, which truly means to give up my right for revenge or retaliation. Moving forward. Learning from everything that happened. As a wounded leader, reaching out to help others in need was perhaps the most important element.

As a leader, did you ever feel like giving up? How did you overcome that feeling?

Oh yes. "*Weeping endures for the night, but joy comes in the morning.*" This verse means that we sometimes only have the wherewithal to simply put one foot in front of the other, hoping the light of day emerges. Showing up, regardless of how we feel at the time, is 90 percent of the answer. It is important to be busy, all the while knowing that, sooner or later, I am going to have to confront the pain in times of silence and meditation before God.

Dealing with the pain is like the function of a ratchet wrench. If I am going to loosen a bolt, I first have to do the "click-click-click" to get the wrench in place to experience the *lefty/loosey.* The "click-click-click" may be viewed by some as a backwards move. But it is absolutely important to the forward move, when one looks at the purpose and function of the ratchet wrench. It simply means that I must step back, lean into the pain, and let

God do his work in me, taking the knowledge I have, crushing me, so that wisdom can become a part of my way of life.

How has your leadership made a difference in the lives of others?

Occasionally a letter arrives, or an email or text is received that has been written by someone expressing gratitude for something I have said or done. It's like God briefly pulls the curtain back to give us a glimpse of the impact our life has had on others. For me, it's like jet fuel for the next six months.

Can you talk about an individual or a situation that helped you realize that you were making a positive difference as a leader?

I had the opportunity to return to a little church in Baltimore where I had served twenty-five years earlier. The people told stories of me visiting them in the hospital, or being there for them when their son or daughter had committed suicide or was on drugs. The memories of visiting families after a drive-by shooting had put bullet holes throughout their home. I remember being at the home with the family of a parent on his or her deathbed. I then realized that living life with people in an authentic manner was important—celebrating with them in their high times and grieving with them in their low times.

Do you consider resilience to be more physical, emotional, or a combination of both?

Combination of both. Vince Lombardi once told his players, "Fatigue makes cowards of us all." That's why he demanded that the players be in their hotel rooms by 10 pm the night before a game. Vince was stating that the physical and the emotional are connected in so many ways.

I have discovered that, especially as I get older, I am healthier as the years go by. Yes, in some ways, I don't have quite as much stamina, but I have grown accustomed to the signals from my body that I ignored when younger.

What advice do you have for individuals in positions of leadership to help them stand strong during times of adversity?

Get to know the power and presence of the One that created us. When we ask to be filled, He is faithful to fill us. "When you are in the jar, you can't read the label." Find trusted people to help read the label for you. "In the multitude of counselors there is safety." "When you get specific, you can become terrific." Get specific about what's happening. Thinking generally will not solve the issue.

JOEL'S KEYS TO RESILIENCY

1. **Make your health a priority. Rest when you need it.**
2. **"Show up," even if you don't feel like it.**
3. **Find trusted counselors to advise you.**
4. **What specifically will you do in response to what you just read in this interview? Set a goal.**

CHAPTER 11

ORGANIZATION

About once a year, I conduct an inventory at home that includes the garage, closets, drawers, and workshop, and realize that they contain items which are no longer needed. Then, I grab three boxes to fill with items I want to keep, items I want to give away, and items I want to throw away. I confess that letting go of the past is challenging. I mean, who knows when I might need a sweater that is now two sizes too small or a shoebox full of dog-eared baseball cards? But emotional entanglements eventually yield to reason, and my home is once again free from clutter.

How does a clean closet relate to resilience? Clutter creates confusion, wastes time, and prevents anything new from occurring in a particular space. Often, we are frustrated or running late because we can't find an item of clothing, a tool, or some piece of sporting gear needed in the moment. Clutter increases stress and therefore reduces resilience. Plainly put, clutter kills.

I was once hired to provide coaching services for a family physician who struggled to maintain proper records, be on time for appointments, and provide meaningful feedback to his office staff. I had met this gentleman several times at events outside of his office and he was always pleasant, focused, and had a great sense of humor. This made it hard to understand the struggles that his office manager described during our initial conversation.

Upon arriving at the doctor's practice, I walked through the spacious waiting room and then into his personal office. I was shocked to see that every square inch of table, desk, shelf, and cupboard space was covered in tan manila file folders, stacked between one and three feet high. The doctor literally had to stand and reach over several of the monstrous piles on his desk just to shake my hand. The discussion that followed seemed like something from a comedy skit, with both of us peeking around files, vainly trying to make eye contact.

Naturally, I raised the issue of the clutter and learned that he kept files for patients who had died twenty years earlier. As so many hoarders do, he vehemently declared that he "knew exactly where everything was." Though I tried my best, I could not get him to remove or even organize the clutter, so he continued his crazy approach of record keeping. Unfortunately but predictably, his practice continued its downward spiral, and thus a good doctor was gradually removed from positions of leadership on committees due to his disorganization, delays, and missed deadlines.

Two Types of Clutter

There are two primary types of clutter. The first, physical, is the easiest to spot and address. If you can no longer park a car in your garage due to all the clutter, it's time for a yard sale. If your kitchen pantry looks like a Picasso painting, take an hour or two and put like things with like things. This holds true for attics, basements, and storage areas of all kinds.

The second type of clutter, emotional (or mental), is more important to address than physical. Much like the doctor's office, emotional clutter comes from holding onto things from the past and present, or worrying about things in the future that we don't need. This sort of "baggage" may be picked up at any stage of life, often starting very young. Traumatic events, such as the divorce of parents, death of a loved one, or any type of abuse, become a filter through which much of life is then viewed and interpreted.

Of course, we all experience a wide variety of wounds along life's path, including those from family, friends, significant others, supervisors, peers, subordinates, and many others. These disappointments, whether large or small, may come in early childhood, middle school, higher education, on the job, and certainly in all sorts of relational situations.

While the variations are endless, there are a few basic categories of these soul-shifting situations that cause us pain, anger, or fear:

- Betrayal: someone you trusted let you down.

- Unfairness: you suffered some sort of injustice.

- Humiliation: you were severely embarrassed.

- Abandonment: someone left you when you needed them.

- Rejection: you were unwanted or passed over.

Again, everyone has experienced one or more of these afflictions. Unless deliberate efforts have been made to get rid of them, they may still be cluttering up our emotional or mental closets. While uncomfortable or unpleasant experiences are universal, not everyone makes the attempt to remove them and make room for new thoughts, increased confidence, and healthy relationships.

I have had my share of disappointments, starting early in life. As a young child, I accompanied my parents to a county fair which was as exciting as it was intimidating. At one point, my mother and father each thought that the other was watching over me and went separate ways, leaving me alone in a crowd of strangers. I was terrified! Later in life, high school was a mixed bag of highs and lows, with plenty of rejection to go around. After I launched my business, I watched trusted employees walk off with major clients of mine. Once I made a sizable loan to a friend which prevented him from losing his house, only to have him refuse to repay me. It has taken time and effort to offload these negative experiences, but it has been well worth it.

Resilience and Clutter

Clutter lowers our resilience by increasing stress, wasting time, and exhausting resources. Whether stocking supplies for a hospital operating room or searching for paint rollers for home projects, if you can't find what you need when you need it, you have two choices: postpone your project or purchase additional supplies. In most instances, a bathroom wall can be painted a few days later; however, when a patient is being wheeled into surgery, there are no excuses for a lack of scalpels, sutures, or gauze. One of my associates, Steven, is an expert in process improvement and works with healthcare organizations to identify waste and organizational clutter. In one hospital system, he discovered that their operating rooms resourced three separate storage areas without any organized process to keep track of supplies. They also had several different people tasked with ordering supplies, so they constantly had an overabundance of some items while running dangerously low on others.

When it comes to mental clutter, it is important to know that our brains can be overloaded, just like that hospital storage locker. If we aren't burdened by something from our past, we might be consumed with worry about the future instead. In the meantime, we try to carry way too many projects, tasks, deadlines, etc. in our mind, but all that data soon jumbles together, leaving us mentally scrambled and emotionally exhausted. Clutter must be eliminated by using some electronic device to help keep it all straight, or by the tried-and-true method of keeping a calendar or a written list of tasks, issues, and timelines.

Early in my career, I always kept a legal pad on my desk, checking it every morning before I did anything else. I would write down everything that needed to be accomplished and categorize the items as either A, B, or C. The A items were those that were the most important and most urgent. I made sure to put maximum effort into those items. The B items were those that were important, but not as urgent. *If* I completed the tasks on the A list, then I would move onto the B items. The C items were those that were things that needed to be done at some point, but were not as important or urgent as the others. I would spend time on the C items only after the others were addressed.

The beautiful thing is that using a simple system trains your mind about how to categorize and prioritize various aspects of your work and home life. Creating lists results in a significant reduction in stress, a high degree of focus, a limited amount of wasted time, and as a result, much higher resilience.

Decluttered Leadership

Once we organize our physical space or personal schedule, it becomes much easier to manage and avoid day-to-day clutter. But how do you get rid of emotional clutter, especially when it stems from something in the past? While it may not be easy, it is relatively simple. I'm happy to say that, in most instances where I have been lied to, cheated, or mistreated, I got over it relatively quickly and moved forward. Here are some keys that always work for me:

- Move quickly past a stage of denial and simply accept that something negative happened.

- Talk about the situation and how you feel with a trusted friend or counselor.

- If possible, let the offending party know how their actions impacted you.

- Learn from it and don't repeat the same mistake again.

- Forgive the one that hurt, cheated, offended you.

This last bullet might be the hardest, but it is critically important. Corrie Ten Boom explained the power of this concept when she said, "to forgive is to set a prisoner free and then discover that the prisoner was you." Keep in mind that forgiveness does not mean that what someone did was, is, or ever will be okay. On the contrary, those that wrong us must live with their decision, and it is highly likely that sowing and reaping, or karma, or the principle that "what comes around goes around" will sneak up and whack them. The beautiful thing about forgiveness is that it allows us to toss the offender's lousy actions out of our mental and emotional closet, so that we can move forward without dragging all that negativity with us.

It is also important to learn from these negative experiences and avoid repeating the same mistakes. I've had some former employees return with hat in hand, asking to be reinstated with my company. While I forgave them for their former actions, I did not allow them back on the team.

Here is an important truth that can help you leave negative experiences behind you and increase resilience: your identity is not what you did on your worst day, nor is it what someone else did to you on their worst day.

Resilient leaders know how to leave the past in the past and move forward just a bit wiser than before.

POINTS TO PONDER

1. Do you allow physical clutter to build up in your workplace or home? If so, how might that impact your resilience?

2. Do you allow mental clutter to build up about your work, home or personal life? If so, how might that impact your resilience?

3. Which strategies can you employ to reduce clutter in your life?

4. What specifically will you do in response to what you just read in this chapter? Set a goal.

INTERVIEW WITH A
RESILIENT LEADER:
MIKE JEFFS

Sunshine Coast, Queensland, Australia

Position: Former CEO of Network Communications

Professional: Operated a family business called Network Communications, which was one of the largest cell phone dealership organizations in Australia. We also run Australia's only home-grown Inspirational Channel which is both a broadcaster and VOD platform known as GOOD.

Personal: Married to Vivian with three sons and now have seven grandchildren.

What was your first leadership role?

My first leadership role was straight out of high school, where I went to work in a bank and at the age of nineteen was appointed as a senior teller. Since then, I have always been in a position of senior management in various employment positions.

What did you learn from those early experiences?

The most powerful/significant life lesson I have discovered is found in this saying: "*The test is not the test.*" As a leader, on any given day you will face tests and challenges, but the actual test is not the test, but how you respond to that test or challenge is the real test.

The most challenging part of leadership is:

Is carrying the weight of responsibility with being a leader, there is no off switch, it comes with the territory.

What are the habits or practices that help you remain positive, engaged, effective, and resilient?

The best definition of leadership I have ever come across is this: "The best leaders were not risk takers, more visionary, and more creative than their comparisons, they were just more disciplined." After fifty years of being in management leadership positions, this definition hits the nail on the head, because whether it is leading a team or pursing a vision, if you are not disciplined in the process, there will be struggle and heartache, whereas a disciplined leader is one that others will follow gladly because they know that he or she walks the walk and talks the talk.

Describe a tough time that you endured as a leader.

One example of this was in the early days of establishing Network Communications. One of our competitors was making false statements that even our customers were concerned about. This was very upsetting to me and all our staff as it had the potential to do great harm to our company.

How did you overcome that tough time?

Some of my staff wanted me to confront this person, but instead, I ended up in front of our competitor's building and praying a blessing over their organization.

So, the next day I told all my staff what I had done, and not to give any further thought to what others were saying or doing but rather focus on building our own business. This we did and soon became one of the largest cell phone distributors in our nation.

As a leader, did you ever feel like giving up?

If I'm totally honest, there are many times that I wondered if it is all worth it. Essentially, why not call it a day and take up fishing or golf or something, but any leader worth his or her salt must persevere. These challenging moments become defining moments and, eventually, you look back and appreciate why you had to go through what you did.

How has your leadership made a difference in the lives of others?

Leadership is all about influence, and a good leader leaves a heritage or legacy that is marked by goodness, such as positive outcomes, a successful organization, appreciation of others, investing into the lives of others that positively impact the communities in which they live. At the end of the day, people are far more important than profits, and leaders that live by this value system will achieve exceptional outcomes.

Can you talk about an individual or a situation that helped you realize that you were making a positive difference as a leader?

During Covid and living in Australia, we had an extensive lockdown period, so I used that opportunity to get bike fit and rode almost every day for a two year period. This allowed me to take part in a charity ride organized by Compassion Australia—so at the ripe old age of seventy-two, I was part of a forty member team that cycled from one side of Australia to the other (2600 miles) and, as a result, raised over $1 million to give children in the developing world a hope and a future they would otherwise never have. It was a very demanding and grueling ride, and the toughest physical undertaking I have ever done—but each day we began by reading a story of one of the Compassion children we were riding for, knowing our efforts each day was making a huge difference in their lives. I also mention this because as leaders, you are never too old to dream a new dream or take on a challenge that you think is beyond you—it just takes desire and the determination to see it through, and in so doing you will impact more lives than you ever thought possible.

Do you consider resilience to be more physical, emotional, or a combination of both?

Resilience is a necessary attribute in any leader's life, as it just comes with the territory of being a leader, and my perception is that it is a case of resilience, perseverance, and determination—these three attributes are necessary qualifications of being a leader who will go the distance and not quit no matter how tough the going gets. I would agree that resilience is a combination of both the physical and the emotional and, as a person of faith,

I would add that there is also a spiritual component as well.

What advice do you have for individuals in positions of leadership to help them stand strong during times of adversity?

There is a quote from Norman Vincent Peale that is one that I always default to in times of challenge and adversity, which ties in beautifully with the "Test is not the Test" Principle: *Any fact facing us is not as important as our attitude toward it, for that determines our success or failure.*

Lastly, treat your leadership role as an adventure, because when you do, you will discover truths and depths of understanding that you never dreamed possible.

MIKE'S KEYS TO RESILIENCY

1. Maintain a positive attitude during times of stress.

2. Push yourself in order to find your limits.

3. Don't return evil for evil. Take the high road.

4. What specifically will you do in response to what you just read in this interview? Set a goal.

CHAPTER 12

COURAGE

First things first. Courage is not the *absence* of fear, but rather the ability to stay on course *despite* the fear. In other words, leaders may feel afraid or anxious in many situations, but successful leaders push past the fear, think clearly, and choose courses of action that lead to success. Every time we effectively face and overcome our fears, large or small, we gain new levels of confidence and resilience.

Courage: Past and Present

Since courage is the capacity to overcome fear, it is fascinating to consider how the term 'fear' has evolved.

In Old English, the word fear meant "sudden danger, peril, or sneak attack." This suggests a person wandering through Sherwood Forest and being assaulted by a pack of long-haired, blue-faced savages. Without the proper response, that wanderer will lose life or limb; he must choose to hide, start running, or grab a sword and fight.

Contrast the etymology with our modern dictionary entry: now, 'fear' is defined as "a distressing emotion, aroused by impending danger, evil or pain *whether the threat is real or imagined*." In today's world, our bodies respond just as they did centuries ago, except the cause of the anxiety is more likely public speaking, a first date, or being summoned to the boss's office. The difference between the old and new definitions is significant, yet the human body's physiological response is the same in either scenario. This means that, if we allow fear to rule our thinking, our bodies will kick into fight-flight-or-freeze mode, even though we are not in any sort of actual danger. Hence courage is necessary in every situation that causes us even a small level of anxiety.

The Struggle is Real

The fears faced by those in leadership come in all sizes and forms. I once coached an executive in the medical field to overcome his fear of public speaking. This was crucial to his success because a significant portion of his duties involved speaking to his Board of Directors as well as large groups of employees. In his case, the solution was two-fold. First, we would sit and talk about his long-term vision for his company and family, reaching the understanding that his work was essential for both to succeed. This provided him with a purpose to endure the stress of the speeches. Second, it involved organizing his thoughts into bullet point form, practicing his presentations until he could glance at his notes without reading them, and then simply show up to make the speech regardless of how nervous he felt inside.

It took more than a year before public speaking no longer intimidated him. But since he experienced paralyzing fear for so long, could he be considered courageous? Absolutely! He never gave up, and never allowed fear to stop him from making a presentation. There were times when he had to make a quick trip to the restroom before speaking…but he always came back to the podium, which was a very courageous thing to do.

Both fear and courage are highly contagious, so this gentleman's courage in learning to speak publicly had a positive impact on hundreds of employees who were emboldened during the challenging times their organization faced. When he spoke, his sincerity convinced the team members that all would be well in the future.

Overcome Your Fear

There have been times in my career when an assignment was out of my comfort zone. In one instance, it was way out. Just over twenty-five years ago, I was invited to come to Africa to participate in a most unusual project. The President of the nation of Benin wanted to provide the best possible life for the citizens of that country and requested some help. He described the project in the following terms:

"I need to know how to show the love of God, in tangible ways, to the five and a half million citizens of our nation."

One of my associates, James Glenn, and I boarded a plane and finally landed in Africa more than thirty hours later to take on this daunting task. Naturally, we were thrust into a foreign culture , and jet lag hit us both hard. We learned that we would be leading a group of some two hundred international business leaders in the project, and we had little time to prepare our strategy. I recall James and I sitting in a small *cabana*, wracking our brains, as antelope, mongoose, and other native creatures wandered by. Here is my confession: I was scared. Since there was no "fight" option, I strongly considered the "flight" option—as in, catching a ride back to the airport and going home. Feeling somewhat trapped, we began to talk about possibilities, strategies, and how to organize the human resources which we had to work with.

Eventually, it occurred to us that we had been successful in assisting small companies to grow and prosper, and we had been successful assisting very large companies grow and prosper, so if we viewed the entire nation of Benin as simply a huge organization and applied the same processes we had used on others, it just might work.

In the week that followed, we organized the business leaders into fifteen groups, each focused on a single aspect of national wellbeing, including transportation, clean water, tourism, community development, and technology. Each group identified one person who was willing and able to serve as facilitator for the subproject. We called those individuals "Champions." By the time my friend and I got back on the plane for home, multiple projects were underway, and many had a lasting impact on that wonderful nation. Sometimes, you just must show up to defeat your fears, and further develop your resilience for what comes next.

Many years before our trip to Africa, I learned the value of remaining calm in highly stressful situations. In my late twenties, I worked as a lumberjack in northern Michigan, leading a small crew of tree cutters armed with chainsaws and double-edged axes. The work was enjoyable but dangerous, with multiple injuries inflicted by falling trees, and serious cuts from the saws and axes.

One day, Tony, a member of our team, was cutting a tree with his axe, and made a short hit—he leaned too far back, and the blade only nicked the trunk. This sent the blade on a downward angle, straight down onto Tony's foot, cutting deep enough to sever his tendons. He screamed and pulled off his boot, revealing a white sock rapidly turning crimson.

The challenge was that we were some twenty miles away from Traverse City, where we could get medical help. We put pressure on the wound and loaded everyone into the work truck, laying Tony across our laps so one of my crew could elevate his foot.

The drive into town was incredibly stressful, as Tony's life literally hung in the balance. During that trip, I recall being laser-focused on going as fast as possible without endangering the entire crew. When we finally arrived at the hospital, we carried Tony in, yelling for help. In minutes, a host of angels in white surrounded us, rushing Tony into an ER room. I recall standing next to him, his face drained of color, trying to keep the young lumberjack calm. Finally, a surgeon came in and began the laborious process of reattaching Tony's tendons and repairing his mangled foot.

Before the surgeon began his work, he looked at me, suggesting that I should sit down. He said, "You did your job, you got him here alive. Let me take over now."

Only then did I realize what *I* must have looked like, covered in Tony's blood, likely in mild shock myself. I stumbled out of the room, found the nearest chair, and collapsed. Once I realized that I could hand off the responsibility for Tony's wellbeing, my body began to shake, and I was completely exhausted. In the end, Tony's foot was repaired, but his days as a lumberjack were over. What I learned from that situation is that, in the most stressful situations, if we don't panic, we can succeed.

Never panic. Plan. Act. Succeed.

I want to emphasize that courage is shown in many ways by diverse people. Courage is obviously found in the heroic actions of law enforcement officers, firefighters pulling victims from burning buildings, and members of the armed forces tasked with rescuing hostages from terrorists. However, courage is also shown in countless invisible acts. Consider the father that gets up early and works late to feed his family. Or the single mother, raising three children on her own. Courage comes in all shapes, sizes, colors, and actions. Every act of courage, every triumph over our fears, builds resilience.

Strategies for Building Courage

Courage and resilience are qualities that can be developed. Here are a few strategies that have worked for me:

When faced with a challenging situation, ask:

- What are the pros and cons of acting on this situation?
- Are my concerns real or imaginary?
- What is the worst that could happen?
- What is the best that could happen?

Address conflicts quickly, before they grow.

- Inner conflicts—process the available information, then make a decision.
- Conflicts with others—let them go, if possible. If not possible, then address them quickly.
- Irreconcilable conflicts—let them go.

Face your fears:

- Express yourself—speak up for your convictions when necessary.
- Remember your purpose and what is at stake to help you push past your fears.
- Get sufficient rest, so that you can think clearly.
- Face your fears, don't run from them.

Each time we face an intimidating situation and overcome it, we grow in courage, confidence, and resilience.

POINTS TO PONDER

1. Describe a situation that you find intimidating or that causes you some degree of anxiety.

2. Identify some steps you can take to better handle the situation[s].

3. How will your resilience grow if you successfully address the situation[s]?

4. What specifically will you do in response to what you just read in this chapter? Set a goal.

HEATHER FREDERICK

Hemlock, Michigan, USA

Position: President/CEO Cornerstone Fabricating and Construction

Professional: Since the age of 18, I've worked in administrative positions. In 1998, I started working at Cornerstone as an assistant to the Controller. I then moved up in the organization in different management positions until in 2017, when I became the company's President/CEO.

Personal: Married with two grown children.

What was your first leadership role?

When I moved into the role as CFO, I was also oversee-ing the HR/Accounting Department. This was a small group of three to four people. In 2017, when I stepped into the leadership role for the entire company, we had just over 40 employees.

What did you learn from those early experiences?

I learned that communication is the key. One thing with communicating, especially in conversations where clarity is needed, is not to assume, but ask questions. Also, don't react out of anger or frustration, but take 24 hours to think about the situation and assess everything before you respond.

The most challenging part of leadership is:

Working together during a difficult situation alongside individuals with strong personalities who believe their way is the only way. At times, people can only see things from one perspective and aren't willing to look at it from another.

As a leader, what are the habits or practices that help you remain positive, engaged, effective, and resilient?

For me, it's important to continue to pursue becoming a great leader. You can always learn something new, if you choose to. I don't want to become stagnant, so I engage in reading, watching videos, or listening to podcasts and then try implementing those skills into my life so I can grow even more.

Describe a tough time you endured as a leader.

The toughest time for me was stepping into the role as the leader of the company and developing trust with the employees. I didn't have a vision, mission statement or values established yet, nor even a team. I knew I needed these, but didn't know how to develop any of it.

How did you overcome that tough time?

Prayed and trusted God to bring me the answer and He did by connecting me with Brian, Kathy and the team at Molitor International. Total life and game-changer for me personally, as well as for the company.

As a leader, did you ever feel like giving up? How did you overcome that feeling?

Definitely felt like giving up, especially at the beginning of developing the team. I had such a great support system, not only from Brian and Kathy, but also family and close friends who spoke truth into my life and provided encouragement.

How has your leadership made a difference in the lives of others?

I believe implementing my training and development program has brought a positive outlook to the team and other employees. Everyone can see and feel the change in the company and in the team leaders. The toxicity and low employee morale has disappeared.

Can you talk about an individual or a situation that helped you know you were making a positive difference as a leader?

Employees will come to me and personally thank me, sharing how they see and feel a difference—not only in the company but in overall employee morale. These are long time employees, 10–15, even 20 years invested in the company. They were here when things were toxic and chaotic, but even they feel encouraged by the change… so this is huge.

Do you consider resilience to be more physical, emotional, or a combination of both?

I believe it's a combination of both.

What advice do you have for individuals in positions of leadership to help them stand strong during times of adversity?

Keep the lines of communication open with your team. Be honest with yourself and your team. Don't give up.

Have a support system outside of the company who can give you a different perspective and who will be gracefully honest with you.

HEATHER'S KEYS TO RESILIENCY

1. Be patient with your career and learn as much as possible at each level.

2. Get help from experts when needed. You don't have to have all the answers.

3. Build a cohesive team to carry the load.

4. What specifically will you do in response to what you just read in this interview? Set a goal.

CHAPTER 13

INTEGRITY

While there are multiple variations of the definition of "integrity," I have always presented it this way: *A person of integrity is one that has clearly defined positive standards, ethics, and values that are demonstrated without compromise.* Please note that the word "perfection" is absent from my definition, for one simple reason—none of us go through life without falling short in word, thought, or deed. To me, integrity is a noble goal that we seek to achieve each day, rather than an ultimate destination.

The connection between integrity and resilience is profound. When we live lives of integrity or wholeness, it allows us to avoid the inner conflicts that come with compromise. Integrity helps us to deal with difficult subjects, speak the truth, and confront challenges without fear that some hidden secret may be discovered, to the detriment of our credibility.

Integrity is quantified and measured by adherence to standards of behavior that are generally accepted as good within a society, company, or family. Self-control, honesty, and fairness are several of the positive standards generally considered admirable. In today's world, there are regular attempts at redefining societal standards of what is acceptable or unacceptable. However, I remain convinced that a majority still embrace some very foundational truths, values, and standards of right and wrong.

Integrity Traps

Over the years, I made a list of traps that caught men and women in positions of leadership. These afflicted solid individuals who either suffered from character flaws or simply had momentary lapses in judgement. In either case, careless words or actions limited their careers and, in some cases, cost them their jobs.

I converted the traps and pitfalls into a set of "L" words to make them easier to remember. In no specific order, they are:

Loot. Many have fallen into the trap of chasing riches rather than purpose. Wealth comes through hard work, a few breaks, and a solid plan. Those who try to take shortcuts end up compromising some aspect of their integrity along the way, and ultimately get caught. I once counseled a high-level executive who was dismissed because he knowingly overstated his travel expenses. He did this despite having an annual compensation package just shy of seven figures. His greed for a few hundred dollars each month ultimately cost him millions of dollars in compensation and ruined his reputation.

Lust. Sex is one of the great pleasures in life, but it has disastrous consequences if you have it with the wrong person, or in the wrong place, or at the wrong time. Countless careers and marriages have been cut short by office romances or other indiscretions committed by lonely traveling leaders and by those who lost focus during the workday.

Losing it. Unbridled anger, loud outbursts, yelling, and other tantrum-like behavior may or may not cost one their job, but it certainly will limit opportunities for promotion. Angry, uncontrolled people aren't trusted to remain cool in the face of a storm and are rarely given the tiller to steer.

Leverage. The misuse of power is one of the most destructive ways to show a lack of integrity. It manifests when someone in authority manipulates, threatens, or otherwise abuses those under his or her leadership. Power hungry individuals may rise to a certain level using these twisted techniques, but they rarely stay there.

Loose Lips. As an executive coach, I earn my living by learning the deepest secrets of high-ranking people in business, government, education, and ministry, and then help them make sense of the world around them. It is my practice to never discuss what is said to me in private with anyone, including my wife or other family members. I have discovered that one of the deadliest sins of those seeking a promotion to be talking too much. The old saying that "loose lips sink ships" holds true today, except that they now sink careers and credibility.

Lying. There are people in this world that have brilliant ideas, can solve complex problems, and can make speeches that rival MLK, but struggle to simply tell the truth. This lack of integrity soon catches up with them and causes others to distrust and minimize their contributions.

These traps share one thing in common: they compromise the reputation of the leader, cloud his or her conscience, and reduce resilience. None of them are worth the consequences.

A Trap is a Trap, Large or Small

Many years ago, I was leading a leadership seminar at a high-end conference center in Louisville, Kentucky. The topics covered included communication, listening skills, shared decision making, and *integrity*. During lunch hour, I made my usual escape to my room to recharge, prepare notes for the afternoon session, and grab a quick bite to eat. As I approached the door to my room,

I passed by the maid cart and noticed small bottles of mouthwash on top of the cart. Since I was flying a great deal in those days, having travel-size toiletries was a real plus, so I grabbed a bottle without thinking and began to step into my half-open door. Just then, a stern and booming voice called out, "What do you want?" I turned to see a very angry maid, about half my size, standing there. I froze instantly, knowing that I'd been caught taking something that wasn't mine. With arms crossed, the woman glared at me, waiting. Unsure of the best course of action, I stepped into my room, letting the door slam behind me.

Once inside, I fumed at the nerve of that maid who dared to confront me, an "important" businessman, over a tiny bottle of mouthwash. I considered calling her boss and reporting her for such an offense. Walking into the bathroom to set down my ill-gotten gain, I looked in the mirror and saw…me. The "important" businessman whose goal that day was to teach high-level leaders about the importance of integrity, standing there with a stolen object.

In seconds, I was crushed, embarrassed, and knew that I was in the wrong. So, I walked back to my door and opened it gingerly, hoping that she had moved down the hallway. No such luck. There she stood.

Like a scolded child, I walked to the maid and handed over the contraband. "I am truly sorry," I apologized, with downturned eyes. "I never should have touched anything on your cart. Please forgive me." After a moment, a broad smile came over her face and she patted my arm, saying, "That's all right, baby. We all make mistakes."

It has been said that "everyone has his price", meaning that each of us will compromise if the reward is big enough. I don't know if this is universally true, but I do know that, on that fateful day, I nearly squandered my integrity for twenty-five cents worth of mouthwash. Lesson learned.

Avoiding the Traps

While no one gets it right every day of our lives, there are some ways to safeguard your integrity from the pitfalls and traps that wait for unsuspecting leaders. Here are some recommendations:

- Establish personal standards. Decide on what is right, wrong, acceptable, and unacceptable behaviors.

- Anticipate challenges to your standards. The best way to get out of a trap is to never get caught in one to begin with. Think about what may go wrong, which situations you need to avoid, and stay away from people or places where potential traps could be found.

- Develop strategies to maintain your standards. For example, if you travel for your work, take along a good book to occupy your evenings rather than spending time in the hotel bar.

- Exercise self-control. Say no to yourself when needed. It is worth it.

- Never compromise your standards. Refuse to buy into the "just once won't hurt" theory of life. "Just once" could be enough to cancel out a lifetime of character building.

Ways to Show Integrity

Don't reject these principles because they are so simple—
it is often the most basic concepts in life that result in
success. If you want to be known as a person of integrity,
the following actions will serve you well:

- Be gracefully honest. Don't sugar coat your communication. Respect others enough to tell them the
  truth, whether the news is good or bad.

- Give credit to others when it is due. Never take
  credit for the work or accomplishment of others.

- Admit your mistakes. Never try to hide or cover up
  errors. Get them out in the open, deal with them,
  and then move on.

- Treat others fairly and consistently. Favoritism at
  work or in the home divides team members and
  shows a lack of basic fairness on the part of a leader.

- Speak *about* others as you would speak *to* them.
  Talking about others behind their backs shows a
  lack of integrity. If there are issues with coworkers

or team members, then go to them and resolve the issues face-to-face.

- Remain committed to your word. If you say that you will do something, do it.

- Guard information that has been shared in confidence. Never share confidential information with others. Doing so ruins relationships and destroys credibility.

There is something very powerful about having a clear conscience. By this, I mean that a leader absolutely must not be involved in underhanded deals, compromising positions, or be forced to waste time hiding dirty words or deeds from others. Having a clear conscience is truly a key to resilience, because it frees up all of a leader's energy to focus on the mission without concern about damage control or some scandal that could erupt at any moment.

POINTS TO PONDER

1. Do you have clear standards that guide your life and work? If so, what are they?

2. Which of the traps identified in this chapter are you most likely to get caught in?

3. What sort of strategy can you employ to protect yourself from the trap?

4. What specifically will you do in response to what you just read in this chapter? Set a goal.

INTERVIEW WITH A RESILIENT LEADER:

VIRGINIA PALINSKY

Saginaw, Michigan, USA

Position: Chief Financial Officer Hausbeck Pickle Company

Professional: My first professional job was at King Par Corporation as a Staff Accountant. Within a year, I became the Assistant Controller and then became the Controller five years later. I worked for King Par for ten years before going to Eastman International, which was a similar business to King Par in the Sporting Goods Industry. After six years, I left for a position at Hausbeck

Pickle Company, a manufacturer of packaged pickles and peppers, as their CFO/Controller.

Personal: I've been married for 30 years to my husband, Curtis. I have two children, Jessica (son-in-law Chad) and Jacob, as well as two grandchildren, Madelyn and Cade.

* * *

What was your first leadership role?

My first leadership role was as Assistant Controller at King Par. I really didn't know what leadership was at the age of 24. I was hungry to learn and enjoyed new challenges. I had a great mentor during those early years of leadership that taught me a lot in terms of accounting and computer information skills. Leadership wasn't discussed much, except for making sure your department hit their goals.

What did you learn from those early experiences?

Well, as my husband would say, I'm a rule follower. Those early days were about doing things the correct way (as

I thought them to be) and holding others accountable. But I naturally also bonded with all the people in my department. We were like family and did things outside of work together. That made it more difficult to hold people accountable, but I found the balance between caring for people and helping them understand when something needed to change. It's almost 20 years later, and I still hold that group dear to my heart. I remember the regrets and mistakes I made, but I'm so thankful for the mercy and forgiveness they all gave me as their leader.

The most challenging part of leadership is:

For me, the most challenging part has been being patient enough to allow others to grow. I found that when I give people the space to grow, it's all the more rewarding to see their development, where they feel engaged and accomplished.

As a leader, what are some habits or practices that help you remain positive, engaged, effective and resilient?

First and foremost, it has been the practice of prayer and meditation every morning. No exceptions! Then, I have some type of daily exercise, stay hydrated, and eat well. I do my best to take a lunch break every day for downtime. At one point, I had to learn to limit distractions with time management and creating healthy boundaries. Playing uplifting music when I'm sitting at my desk does wonders for a calm day. Lastly, practicing gratitude by giving thanks for small wins throughout the day has helped me to stay positive and help others that work with me to stay positive as well.

Describe a tough time you endured as a leader.

I came to work for Hausbeck Pickle Company at the age of 40. Hausbeck Pickle is a wonderful place to work and I'm so blessed to be working for the Hausbeck family, but as with any leadership role, there have been many ups and downs. When the pandemic of Covid-19 came, our leadership team fell apart, choosing to work in silo instead of together. Our relationships were so broken, and our leadership team needed healing. It was then that we engaged Molitor International and they took us through their proven leadership training process. Brian recommended that I be promoted to Executive Vice President [while still serving as CFO] to help reorganize the leadership structure. The workload was heavy, but that never deterred me. In my new role, I had leaders reporting to me from various departments that I did not have direct experience with, so my focus was on leading rather than trying to know each person's duties.

How did you overcome that tough time?

What got me through that difficult time was staying true to myself. I remained confident in who I was and my leadership abilities. I practiced the habits I listed earlier which allowed me to stay focused with positivity. I engaged with leadership training and, because I'm human, there were times when the pressure got too great and I allowed myself to shed a few tears. During those times, I practiced patience with others, and I realized that at times, I'd made mistakes. When I made those mistakes, I learned to go back and ask for forgiveness.

Building trusting relationships was key while holding leaders to the tasks at hand that had to be completed. Even then, the healing among our leadership team came over a three-year period.

As a leader, did you ever feel like giving up? How did you overcome that feeling?

I've felt like giving up on every job I've had. I get to a point where it felt too overwhelming and I would feel like I was not in control of the situation. I wanted to run from it and start fresh with a new company. I overcome that feeling with family, friends, and mentors encouraging me to stick with it. They help me to see the truth about the situation and those times when I *did* leave a company, it wasn't because I gave up. It's important to have those types of people in your life that can help you see what the truth is so you can get past your fears of not being in control of an outcome.

How has your leadership made a difference in the lives of others?

I hope that I have encouraged others to do the best they can in any job they are asked to do. I have done my best to help them find roles that they can be happy in. I was a working mother while I was raising my two children. Because of this, I try to help other working mothers know that there are different seasons in life *and* that the way that looks will be different for every mother. This helps them find the proper balance between work, family and personal life.

Can you talk about an individual or a situation that helped you know you were making a positive difference as a leader?

That would be a former person who worked for me, Russ. We didn't always agree on everything, but we respected one another. We went to a seminar called "Our Community Listens" together. It really helped us both with how to communicate better. He said many times that I was the best manager he has ever had—and that was saying something, given the number of people he's worked for over 50+ years. Russ retired at the age of 70. My previous mentor said I was the "glue" that held the organization together. I do not take compliments very well at work because I feel I'm just doing my job, but as time goes on, I realize that sharing the gifts and talents I have helps everyone and brings me great joy. I want this for everyone.

Do you consider resilience to be more physical, emotional, or a combination of both?

For me, it is more emotional. When difficult times come, I need to be good at self-coaching my mind and knowing when it is time to take a break. I tell myself, "Take a deep breath." Physically, a deep breath helps calm the nervous system and relieves muscle tension. I wish I could have learned yoga early on in my career! So, I guess resilience is physical as well.

What advice do you have for individuals in positions of leadership to help them stand strong during times of adversity?

Always step back and look at the big picture. How are you and others being affected? Then, come back with a plan that reflects your values and creates a solution that shows you have taken everything into consideration. Take care of yourself first both physically and mentally so you can give your best to others.

VIRGINIA'S KEYS TO RESILIENCY

1. Build an effective team around you.

2. Make self-care a high priority in your life.

3. Know when you need a break, and then take time to recharge.

4. What specifically will you do in response to what you just read in this interview? Set a goal.

CHAPTER 14

CONFIDENCE

Remember that we defined resilience as the capacity to face opposition and then bounce back just as good, if not better, than before. One of the contributors to the powerful force of resilience is confidence. Proper application requires much more than "self-confidence," although that is part of it.

Confidence that leads to greater resilience, encompasses confidence in the following parties:

- **Self:** Including your own abilities, insights, experiences, choices, preparation, and talents.

- **Partners:** Peers at work, home, and community that share the collective load.

- **Team members:** Everyone serving under the guidance of the leader.

- **The mission:** Firm belief that the goals being pursued are truly worthy of maximum effort.

To be sure, self-confidence is the foundation of the concept, for if a leader is filled with doubt about his or her abilities, then it will be impossible for others to follow along with any degree of security. Self-confidence must not be confused with arrogance, boasting, or shouting self-affirming slogans into the air. Rather, it is a humble knowing that one's purpose is sound, one's abilities are adequate, and one's preparation is sufficient to face whatever comes.

Confidence in Others

Because leaders need others in order to achieve their goals, it is not sufficient for a leader to simply be confident in him or herself. This confidence must extend to all those who are part of the leader's mission, including coworkers, team members, and family members. Without such confidence, leaders often spend an inordinate amount of time checking up on the performance of others, redirecting efforts, and correcting mistakes. These actions represent a huge amount of wasted effort, which results in low resilience for the leader.

Self-Confidence and Self-Awareness

Self-confidence without a keen sense of self-awareness creates a host of problems for a leader. Self-awareness means that a leader has a clear and unbiased picture of his or her. . .

- Mental state: Beliefs, assumptions, values.

- Emotional state: Feelings, moods, responses.

- Actions: What is done, what is said, how it is said.

There are two extremes to avoid when it comes to self-awareness. The first is *under*valuing or being overly critical of our own abilities, personality, looks, status, or achievements. Humility is a great quality, but it does not mean that we only see deficiencies in ourselves.

Self-criticism creates self-doubt instead of self-confidence, making it very difficult to achieve great things or have any hope of becoming resilient.

The other extreme of self-awareness is seen in the person who vastly *over*values one or more aspect of himself. These clueless individuals stand out from the crowd, but for all the wrong reasons. Since we all have some built-in biases, it is important to not only understand how we see ourselves, but also how we are perceived by those around us Recently, I provided leadership training to Directors and Executives of a Medical Device firm and ran into one of the least self-aware individuals that I've ever met. He was rather homely, yet fancied himself a ladies' man. He was boring, but would corner lower-level managers to pontificate about irrelevant topics. He would tell jokes that no one laughed at, and often attempted to make pithy comments during meetings that were clearly unappreciated. The general response toward him from peers and direct reports was one of annoyance. At one point, I asked if he was interested in some professional feedback on his interactions with others or help with his approach to leadership. His response was telling: "No thanks. I don't really need it." No self-awareness.

Developing Confidence in Self and Others

Confidence, like many leadership attributes, can be developed over time and with the proper plan in place. The following components are essential aspects of a confidence plan:

- Vision: Make sure that the mission is clear and the worthy goals are attainable.

- Preparation of self for the worthy tasks ahead: Once you have set your course and clarified your purpose, then it is time to learn all that you can about your field. This requires study, growth, practice, asking questions of others, finding a mentor, and spending time developing your abilities.

- Selection of solid partners: Be highly selective when you identify and secure high-quality individuals to help you share the load. These must be people whom you trust and enjoy spending time with.

- Preparation of team members: Secure, train, prepare, coach, mentor, appropriately compensate, and motivate those working under your care.

- Keep your conscience clear: Never compromise your standards or wander from your purpose.

With these in place, self-confidence will grow and with it, resilience.

POINTS TO PONDER

1. Do you tend to overestimate or underestimate yourself?

2. Do you have a friend or coworkers that can give you feedback on how you are perceived by others? If so, make a plan to have a gracefully honest conversation with that person.

3. Are you confident in those around you? If not, what needs to change in order for your confidence in them to increase?

4. What specifically will you do in response to what you just read in this chapter? Set a goal.

INTERVIEW WITH A RESILIENT LEADER:

BRIAN D. MOLITOR

Midland, Michigan, USA

Position: Chief Executive Officer of Molitor International

Professional: Founder and CEO Molitor International. Founder of Malachi Global Foundation

Personal: Married to Kathleen with four grown children and seven grandchildren.

What was your first leadership role?

I was the supervisor for a group of lumberjacks in northern Michigan.

What did you learn from those early experiences?

I learned that leadership can be like trying to herd cats. People have their own ideas about how to go about things and if you don't get them working together, things can go very badly. In the case of this forestry crew, we had several individuals severely injured when they deviated from established procedures.

The most challenging part of leadership is:

Finding the balance between developing positive relationships with subordinates and maintaining proper levels of authority to get the work done.

What are the habits or practices that help you remain positive, engaged, effective, and resilient?

I love to work hard and to accomplish challenges in a team environment, so there is a natural enthusiasm that comes from the work itself. Beyond that, I try to let go of disappointments quickly so that I'm not dragging around the past. Finally, my faith plays an important role in whatever work I am doing and helps me find purpose, even when things go wrong.

Describe a tough time that you endured as a leader.

There have been quite a few, but the ones that come to mind deal with the issue of broken trust. I've had a couple of employees abandon me and "steal" clients. Also, I've helped people when they were in deep financial trouble, only to have them renege on repayment.

How did it impact you and/or those around you?

Initially, I was heartbroken and shocked. Honestly, I felt used and taken advantage of. This spilled over onto my wife, who was my confidante, so we were both in bad shape for a while after each instance.

How did you overcome that tough time?

Three keys. First, I took stock of the situation and assessed the damage done. This prevented me from having a strictly emotional response. Second, I talked about how I felt with my wife and others in leadership positions, so I did not bottle it all up. Finally, I forgave the offenders and asked God to keep me from becoming bitter.

Interestingly, the clients eventually came back to me, after discovering that the employee that departed lacked character…big surprise? Also, the financial losses were made back up over a period of time. Things work out eventually if you don't give up.

As a leader, did you ever feel like giving up?

Yes. I always loved working as an entrepreneur, but the downside of the freedom is that there is no safety net under you, financially speaking. I recall some years when, in late November, we had no work on the books for the following year for me or my staff, and those were some dark days. By the grace of God, the phone would ring, often in mid-December, and our calendar would fill up once again.

How did you overcome that feeling?

I never lost the excitement of entrepreneurship nor my faith that, if we stayed the course, it would all work out. Prayer was part of the process as well. Having a supportive wife that endured some of those challenges was extremely important. She is one in a million and has stuck by me in the ups, downs, and sideways of leadership.

How has your leadership made a difference in the lives of others?

I see this as a team answer, as many times we heard back from leaders and employees alike that our training had changed the culture in both their places of business and in their homes. Because we teach principles of leadership and relationship building, many that attended our seminars would report new, positive relationships with spouses and children as a result of applying what we taught them.

Can you talk about an individual or a situation that helped you realize that that you were making a positive difference as a leader?

Perhaps the most profound example of this comes from an organization in Elizabethtown, Kentucky. This union-ized manufacturing plant was scheduled for closure due to two nasty strikes that cost the parent company over $3 million dollars. This would have put two hundred and sixty people out of work, and devastated the community as well. My team and I went to work, training their lead-ers and staff members. Along the way, an amazing thing happened. The plant went from near closure to the best in every bottom-line category, including productivity, quality, profitability, waste reduction, and more. There have been other such stories since then, but this was the first and it helped me know that my theories about organizational success would actually work.

Do you consider resilience to be more physical, emotional, or a combination of both?

I'd say it's 20 percent physical and 80 percent emotional/ mental. When part of your life is spent traveling, eating out, sleeping in different hotels, and public speaking, you need to keep yourself as physically healthy as possible. However, you could be in peak physical shape, but if you lose focus, forget why you are doing what you do, or hit a rough patch and can't shake it from your thinking, then you are in trouble.

What advice do you have for individuals in positions of leadership to help them stand strong during times of adversity?

Start by surrounding yourself with good people that you can trust. Remember why you took the position of leadership in the first place, and then count your blessings that come with the responsibility. Serve others at least as much as you serve yourself, if not more. Trust God, trust yourself, enjoy the ride.

BRIAN'S KEYS TO RESILIENCY

1. Put the needs of others first.

2. Remember, the tallest trees get hit with the strongest wind. As your influence grows, expect resistance and then push past it.

3. Keep your emotions balanced. Nothing lasts forever and even the greatest challenges will pass.

4. What specifically will you do in response to what you just read in this interview? Set a goal.

CHAPTER 15

STEADFASTNESS

I n my travels around the globe, I have met many fascinating individuals, from famous actors to presidents of nations. Despite their diversity of age, gender, race, nationality, education, and experience, they all have one thing in common: failure. In fact, many of them failed multiple times before finally making their mark on the world. Somehow, these individuals found the strength to overcome, adapt, and bounce back from what seemed like catastrophic failures. If life, liberty, and love were easy, there would be no need for the concept of resilience. We would come into this world with everything we require, experience a perfect childhood, marry the love of our life, have perfect children, step into the ideal job, make more money than we need, and find the deepest fulfilment in our leisure pursuits.

Nice thought, but that's not reality.

There is rarely anything perfect about our lives, careers, or relationships, so in any of these important fields, we become comfortable with trying, failing, and getting back up again. For resilient leaders, quitting is not an option unless some endeavor has been proven fruitless or until it is too dangerous to continue down a certain path. So, if you've ever fallen short, outright failed, or felt like giving up, know that you are in excellent company. Let me introduce you to a few of your peers.

Famous Failures

Colonel Harland Sanders is the founder of Kentucky Fried Chicken (KFC) restaurants. His legacy was one of multiple failures until, at the age of sixty-five, he took his now famous chicken recipe and just over $100 and went traveling across country, hoping to find a buyer for his recipe. Over a thousand restaurants rejected him before one finally took a chance on his approach to making chicken dinners. How did it work out? Well, in 1964,

Sanders sold the franchise for $2 million dollars, which is just under $20 million in today's money.

Another resilient leader was Henry Ford, who helped bring transportation to the masses in America and the world. Like Colonel Sanders, Ford experienced several noteworthy failures before he found success. His first company went bankrupt, and his second company failed after feuding with his partners. Fortunately, Mr. Ford was no quitter, and his namesake, the Ford Motor Company, is now worth over $40 billion dollars.

One of the most successful authors in history is J. K. Rowling, but few know that, at one point, she was a single mother living on welfare, trying to support her daughter. Rowling's initial book took years to write and was initially rejected by all the major publishing houses. Fortunately, she never quit, and her net worth today is approximately $1 billion dollars.

Famous actor Keanu Reeves endured many hardships in his early years. After his father abandoned his family, his mother remarried and divorced four separate times. As a young adult, Reeves lost a child and shortly thereafter, his ex-wife was killed in a car accident. However, Keanu did not give up, and has since appeared in nearly eighty full-length movies, including *The Matrix* series and *John Wick*. His charity work is legendary, and the world is a much better place because of his steadfast refusal to quit.

Sylvester Stallone was once homeless, living in the New Jersey Port Authority bus station. While he was writing the script for his now-famous movie *Rocky*, he was forced to sell his dog for $25 just to keep his lights on. Over 1,500 talent scouts rejected him before he finally got his big break and became an international superstar. And yes, he eventually bought his dog back.

One of the most resilient men of all time is the inventor Thomas Edison. He failed over 10,000 times to invent a commercially viable light bulb. But his failures pale in comparison to his successes, and there are still 1,093 patents in his name. When asked about his many failures, Edison responded: *"I have not failed 10,000 times. I have succeeded in proving that those 10,000 ways will not work. When I have eliminated the ways that will not work, I will find the way that will work."*

It is important to note that we have the benefit of hindsight when viewing the legacies of these famous folks. However, when they were living through these difficult times, they had no crystal ball, and there was no guarantee how their stories would end. All that they knew for sure was that they had to keep going, or else walk away from their dreams.

These great individuals are not the only ones who persevered in the face of challenges. Countless stories of courage, steadfastness, and resilience are being written every day, all around the globe. When my wife, Kathleen, was pregnant with our second son, she was placed on bed rest. We were told that otherwise, the odds that our child would not survive the pregnancy were extremely high. The challenge was that she was only three months pregnant at the time, which meant she needed to remain in bed for essentially 23 hours a day for half a year. What made this even more challenging is the fact that we had a very active two-year-old son, and I had recently launched my consulting business, which meant regular out-of-state travel for me. The months crawled by slowly, yet Kathleen remained steadfast, motivated by the vision of bringing another child into the world. Somehow, between extended family making meals, friends helping with our other son, and the grace of God, we made it through. Kathleen's resilience was stronger than that incredible challenge.

When I think about all the wonderful examples of people who faced adversity and yet were resilient enough to continue the journey, I realize that their stories share several themes:

- Each person had a goal or mission that was worth pursuing.
- Each person was willing to endure hardship to achieve their goal.
- Each person overcame doubt and fear to succeed.
- Each person remained faithful to the mission… and never quit.

As I review the list above, I wonder how many potential Henry Fords, Rockys, Colonel Sanders, or Kathleens gave up just short of their goal. How many failed to develop the necessary resilience to persevere, overcome, and succeed? My guess is there are plenty, but that doesn't have to be the case for you. The need for resilient leaders today is immense, and the challenges are many.

You can be counted among those who were tested, who were weary, who wavered, but who ultimately remained steadfast and then bounced back strong.

Failure isn't final…unless you quit.

My advice is simple. Never give up. Never give in. Always believe.

POINTS TO PONDER

1. Have you ever felt like giving up? How did you deal with those feelings?

2. What are some keys to retaining your drive and commitment?

3. What is the outcome of you continuing to push forward in your work, home, or personal life?

4. What specifically will you do in response to what you just read in this chapter? Set a goal.

RESILIENCE: YOU'VE GOT WHAT IT TAKES

L et's take a moment to reflect on all the storms you have endured; all the times that you struggled with finances, relationships, problems and challenges of all sorts; all the missed opportunities, questionable decisions, bad breaks, and other mini hurricanes that threatened to sink you. Despite all these challenges, you are still sailing.

The bumps, bruises, scrapes and scars we carry leave a mark, but rather than signs of failure, these are the signs that we are resilient individuals who took life's best punch and yet never quit. To be clear, none of us made it this far alone. We had help from those around us who reminded us of what we often failed to see in ourselves: drive, determination, courage, love, and so much more. Regardless of whether you are currently on top of the world or feel like you are at the bottom of the heap, your inner strength has brought you this far, and will carry you further, all the way to your final destination.

If today is a great day, filled with victory, then celebrate. If today is a day of great challenge, then focus, find your answers, and get back in the race. Remember all of the great people who shared their stories in this book. These diverse individuals share one profound quality—resilience.

I invite you to take some time with the self-assessment that follows and identify your points of strongest resilience as well as any areas that need some work. Then put together plans to grow in these vital qualities in the years ahead.

You made it this far and you are not going to be stopped. You've got what it takes!

RESILIENCE SELF-ASSESSMENT

Now that we have examined the importance of each of these qualities, take some time to be gracefully honest with yourself by rating where you are in each category today. For additional insights, ask someone who knows and cares about you to rate you as well.

Keep in mind that resilience can increase or decrease over time and depending on circumstances. Allow your initial assessment to serve as a benchmark and then, every so often, come back and rate yourself again. If you apply the principles found in this book, it is highly likely that you will grow in many areas and increase your overall resilience.

Stress Control: Able to effectively manage level of stress from many factors to minimize negative impact on overall health:

1 2 3 4 5 6 7 8 9 10

Purpose/Vision: Can see beyond the moment; not stuck in the present:

1 2 3 4 5 6 7 8 9 10

Balance/Pace: Maintains proper pace and balance in life:

1 2 3 4 5 6 7 8 9 10

Optimism: Has a positive outlook, not hindered by negativity:

1 2 3 4 5 6 7 8 9 10

Self-control: Able to restrain unhealthy desires by the use of reason:

1 2 3 4 5 6 7 8 9 10

Strategy: Remains focused on setting and achieving high level priorities:

1 2 3 4 5 6 7 8 9 10

Crucial Connections: Builds effective relationships with others:

1 2 3 4 5 6 7 8 9 10

Self-Care: Deliberately manages stress, rest, diet, and physical activity:

1 2 3 4 5 6 7 8 9 10

Faith: Trusts in self, teammates, family members and a higher power to provide help in times of need:

1 2 3 4 5 6 7 8 9 10

Organization: Lives and leads unhindered by unnecessary issues:

1 2 3 4 5 6 7 8 9 10

Courage: Overcomes fear and is able to function despite challenges:

1 2 3 4 5 6 7 8 9 10

Integrity: Consistently lives by clear standards; uncompromising:

1 2 3 4 5 6 7 8 9 10

Confidence: Remains self-assured without being arrogant; understands own strengths, weaknesses and motives, as well as the perception of others:

1 2 3 4 5 6 7 8 9 10

Steadfastness: Stays committed to worthy goals despite challenges:

1 2 3 4 5 6 7 8 9 10

Once you have completed your self-assessment, identify which are your strongest qualities and which you want to further develop. Be kind and yet firm with yourself as you set goals for greater resilience. Take one step at a time and watch your progress build.

Enjoy the journey!

ABOUT THE AUTHOR

Brian D. Molitor is Chief Executive Officer of Molitor International, an award-winning company with over thirty-five years of experience providing consulting, training, and coaching services to clients in North America, Australia, Europe, the United Kingdom, the Caribbean, and Africa.

Brian's company specializes in organizational development, change management and the creation of customized training programs. Molitor International's own complete line of training materials cover a wide variety of topics including leadership, team building, interpersonal relationships, communication, trust building, conflict resolution, reconciliation, and problem solving.

Over the years, Mr. Molitor has produced and hosted numerous television series on fatherhood, interpersonal relationships, family building, and leadership. These shows have aired worldwide. Brian has served on many executive boards, including area labor–management committees, a statewide prison ministry, and international businesses.

National and international audiences recognize Mr. Molitor as an expert who cuts through the theories of the day and communicates the practical application of foundational principles necessary for organizational and personal success.

He is also a prolific writer of both fiction and non-fiction and his books are enjoyed by readers around the globe. His first book, *Building Resilient Teams*, explored ways to apply the principles of resilience to create self-supporting and goal-oriented teams in the workplace. His life has been filled with adventure and travel to faraway places including Australia, Africa, the Caribbean, United Kingdom and more. In his younger days, he worked as a lumberjack, semipro football player, factory laborer, and entrepreneur. When he is not fishing in crocodile-infested waters in the Northern Territories or flying over the tundra in Alaska, he is home with his wife of nearly 40 years in Midland, Michigan. Some of his favorite moments are spent reflecting on his four grown children, seven grandchildren, and the grace of God that made it all possible.